LAMP
BACK

LAMP BACK

Plays and Other Grievances

Anthony Hudson

Edited and with an introduction by Kate Bredeson

NORTHWESTERN UNIVERSITY PRESS
EVANSTON, ILLINOIS

Northwestern University Press
www.nupress.northwestern.edu

Printed in the United States of America

10 9 8 7 6 5 4 3 2 1

ISBN 979-8-89948-069-0 (paper)
ISBN 979-8-89948-070-6 (ebook)

Cataloging-in-Publication Data are available from the Library of Congress.

For Linda Baker and Dan Hays

CONTENTS

PREFACE

My ancestors are in plenty of books. Modern history books share stories of my grandmother and her siblings fighting for Siletz's Tribal restoration. My cousin David Gene Lewis's *Tribal Histories of the Willamette Valley* (Ooligan Press, 2023) contains the words and rituals of my great-grandpa's aunts and uncles as they lived the endgame of Manifest Destiny.[1] And in the early twentieth century, white ethnolinguists[2] interviewed us on the Grand Ronde Reservation, trying to preserve our languages—and with them, our cultures—before we were all supposed to die out.[3] Unfortunately for the American project as a whole, we went back on our promise to go extinct. Fortunately—for all Native Americans *and* the survival of humanity, but particularly for me—we're still here, like that Elaine Stritch song.[4] And the trickle-down effects of genocide reveal a silver lining: I'm now the author of a book.

It's a weird thing, having a book. I've only ever read them before. I've spent my life writing, but as someone arguably best known as 1) a performer, 2) an untrained clown, and 3) the whitest woman this side of Lake Oswego,[5] I've reminded people that I'm a writer for the entirety of my

---

1. Now known as *They-ifest Destiny*.
2. These white people had names, I'm sure, but my ancestors simply called most of them "Boston," because that's where many of the academics came from (and because they all looked and sounded the same). Natives have always had a penchant for nicknames and reappropriating language to better suit us. We'll take the words you give us, but we'll make them funnier and work in uncomfortable reminders of every evil thing you've done for the last five hundred years.
3. And become ghosts who torment white people moving into new homes, like in *The Amityville Horror* (1979), *Poltergeist* (1982), *Pet Sematary* (1989), and when I bust out my leaf blower.
4. "I'm Still Here" from Stephen Sondheim's *Follies* (1971).
5. A horrible, wealthy, segregated suburb just southwest of Portland, Oregon.

(mid)career. Perhaps "unscripted" reality television or the eldritch horrors of college improv comedy have convinced the public that plays and drag performances simply materialize out of thin air—as do videos, lectures, manifestos, and stand-up comedy.

I'm gay,[6] in addition to what feels like an endless tessellation of intersecting identities, so obviously high school theater changed my life. But despite occasionally putting on clown armor and managing an obsessive need to process all my private woes, insecurities, and grudges on a public stage, I'm an introvert. I make sense of my surroundings through ~~endless ruminating~~ writing because that's what *Harriet the Spy* (1996) did.[7] When I signed up for theater as a freshman-year elective, our drama teacher, Mrs. Baker, quickly figured me out: "I'm onto you," she told me, after reviewing my class notebook. "You sit there quietly, writing, and nobody knows you're eviscerating us all from your desk. Now I want to see you do that onstage."

I accepted Mrs. Baker's challenge. Introverted and shy, I still wanted to be seen and make people laugh. Among my earliest memories is watching my dad emcee my grandma's eightieth birthday party. His version of comedy consisted of dad jokes—like "playing the sax," in which he fumbled with a plastic grocery sack like it was a saxophone—and I was transfixed by his ability to lead a communal experience with comedy.[8] I would never watch another emcee or speaker without dreaming of becoming one myself. I also liked the idea of acting, but the puppet master[9] quality of an emcee—to be the cruise director for an audience's collective experience—was what I really, really wanted[10] from performance.

Like a screaming drunk girl at a party, I lived for drama. By my senior year, I'd satisfied most of my credit requirements and never left the auditorium, only taking theater classes. I had no school spirit, but I lettered in drama. I played the killer, Justice Lawrence Wargrave, in Agatha Christie's *Ten Little Indians*, proving once and for all that an Indian kid can play

6. Spoiler alert! Ban this book.
7. Rest in peace, Michelle Trachtenberg.
8. *Looking for Tiger Lily* was inspired by—and designed after—the PowerPoint presentations I watched my dad give to white social workers about the Indian Child Welfare Act. I quickly learned how his weaving of humor and facts made white people listen to an Indian man and accept him as a person.
9. "Pull the strings!" (*Ed Wood*, 1994).
10. À la Scary, Sporty, Baby, Posh, and Ginger Spice.

an Irish serial killer. In a more racially insensitive twist, I was Shylock in Shakespeare's *The Merchant of Venice*.[11]

I started reading plays and sought out comedies by queer writers. One day, I somehow pulled an especially magical book off the shelf—*27 Short Plays* by Christopher Durang—and everything changed. I don't remember if I read *Sister Mary Ignatius Explains It All for You* before I sought out Showtime's TV adaptation starring Diane Keaton,[12] or if it happened the other way around; perhaps I simply stumbled through a holy nexus of both curiosity and fate when I reached for his play collection at Borders. Either way, Durang's work became my Bible. I'd never read anything so funny—so presentational, smart, stunted, quick, cruel, and hilarious. Durang's plays were everything I wanted to see. I carried the book with me in my binder every day at school, along with my paper, pens, and Pee-Chee folders. Just a few years before, this was an esteemed honor held by William Peter Blatty's 1971 novel *The Exorcist*.

I grew up watching the comedy troupe Monty Python and its absurdist, Arthurian movie masterpiece *Monty Python and the Holy Grail* (1975). Durang, as a distant cousin of farce and a descendant of the Theater of the Absurd, was the satirical, political queer comedy writer I needed next. As I grew into a weirder teenager and a more insufferable thespian, I began writing plays, and I sought out more work from ancestral queer playwrights, comedians, and agitators: Margaret Cho, Joe Orton, Charles Busch, Eddie Izzard, and John Cameron Mitchell; and, later, John Waters, Sandra Bernhard, Miss Coco Peru, and Valerie Solanas.

Proudly clinging to my drama letter and Heart of the Theater Award, I graduated high school, spent several years hiding from adulthood and working at the mall,[13] went to art school, befriended Jinkx Monsoon[14] and fell in love with drag, and became a clown. It happened naturally after a breakup following my first year of art school and when I could no longer abide a small life. A friend invited me to a drag party, but the only makeup I had was white cream paint from a zombie-themed public health PSA

11. Yes, we can participate in problematic theatrical representation too! This is progress.
12. *Sister Mary Explains It All* (2001), costarring Jennifer Tilly.
13. And I did my time: three years in the world of fine (just *fine*) fragrance as a Bath & Body Works lotionista.
14. A benefit of working at the mall: your dear coworker and soon-to-be-friend Kenny, who also loves *Battlestar Galactica*, invites you over—with a caveat about a "crazy drag queen roommate." The rest is herstory.

I'd made.[15] So my friend[16] and I spackled our faces in whiteface like Euphegenia Doubtfire with Cool Whip. "You look like a Carla," they told me as we were getting ready, and the name took. I figured her last name should be Rossi—to evoke Carlo Rossi, of course—because, like the wine, she's bitter, salty, and belongs on the bottom shelf.[17] After that first party, we started getting invited to others, and then to bar nights, and then to cabarets, and Carla was truly born.

In Portland in the early 2010s, drag was a crucible wherein I could meld all my interests: I could emcee, write my own material, make theater, be pretentious like the performance artists I studied in college, and be funny—all while hiding behind a mask. My queer professors David Eckard and Linda Kliewer challenged me to start bringing my drag into school.[18] And the thing I did for fun during my drunk Lindsay Lohan era of college became my art practice. My thesis mentor, Sarah Sentilles, challenged me to make my drag relevant, and my way of making art became my means for complaining about being Native, biracial, and queer in the whitest city in the United States.

Looking for Tiger Lily is entirely about this. In my first six years as Carla Rossi, and almost anonymously (there was no Anthony Hudson then, only her), fragile white Portlanders booed Carla's Karen-like behavior at bar shows. I realized I needed to explain who I was and why I was painting myself white, so I made *Looking for Tiger Lily* in 2016. Daring to make a show without clown armor—though I opened it as her—I treated my autobiographical solo show as a case study in how pop culture can create someone like me, at the intersection of so many identities.[19] The show helped audiences and organizations see me as more than a drag queen, and my career was launched.

I began touring *Tiger Lily*—and Carla with it—to mostly kind and occasionally bewildered audiences all over the United States and beyond

15. For a contest, which won me $3,000 and an awkward lunch date with Gus Van Sant.

16. Long live Florence Oregon, Carla Rossi's long-lost sister and cofounder of the Tampon Troupe. We called ourselves that because we were white and absorbent.

17. Like my formative trancestor The Lady Chablis, I got my name from a wine bottle (*Midnight in the Garden of Good and Evil*, 1997).

18. After a brief, failed stint at Portland State University immediately after high school, I started art school years later as an illustrator. I wanted to study theater in a university, but I didn't want to take math classes.

19. I blame it *all* on *Peter Pan*.

its invented borders. Created after *Tiger Lily*'s success and charting everything from anti-drag hysteria to the pandemic and its reckonings, the other works in this collection create a narrative about what happens to an introverted young[20] artist who goes from DIY cardboard waves and canoes in cabarets to international expectations and forty airplanes a year. These texts—and particularly *Nobody's going to fund this*—also speak to what happens when we let organizations recolonize us and plant flags in our work for a dangling carrot of opportunity and exposure, all while nonprofits check off equity boxes for funding requirements.[21]

Throughout all of it, and every time I stepped onstage, I imagined the Fool card of the Tarot: take a breath, disregard terror,[22] and step off the cliff. Remember what you wrote—learn it, trust it—and then throw out the book. Add what the audience needs to connect to you in that moment, and do exactly what you need. This is how I played. And for a long time, Carla—my Super Saiyan,[23] me at my most unbearable—made it possible to be loud and fearless and annoying and gross and popular. She's taken me from bars and basement dressing rooms to concert halls and the Venice Biennale. Carla is a funny and dominating personality, and she's perhaps best served raw, improvised, and bitterly in the moment, and my writing is at her core. Her central processing unit, like a cybernetic clown Terminator, is me, sitting with poor posture at my desk—or, more likely, huddling on my bed, or hunched over on the couch, or in the shower, or sweating through a run, or grabbing my phone and opening the Notes app at one in the morning, or actively reading the expression of every single person in the audience in adrenaline-dilated bullet time—and writing.

Today—

(Honestly, I'm nervous to temporally situate what I'm writing *now*, for this book, because I like to think of books as perfect, timeless things, but they're not. They're printed and dated and published. Durang's work is full of references from the time of its writing, and as a teenager, if I wanted in on the joke, I had to look it up. I write in the same way, and . . . oh god this

20. Ahem. Once. At the time.

21. Fortunately, neither equity nor funding (nor nonprofits?) exist at the time of this writing.

22. And red flags, and your intuition, and warnings from your body.

23. In the anime world of *Dragon Ball Z* (1989–1996), a Super Saiyan transformation makes Goku fifty times more powerful. It's sort of like a magical girl transformation, à la *Sailor Moon*, but Carla isn't a magical girl—she's a trash clown.

contextual digression is taking way too long and I haven't said any Indian stuff since the first paragraph and this book is going to feel so out of place in the Native American Studies section and . . .)

Today, I'm in a place[24] where I feel much more capable writing than performing. Carla has been with me for sixteen years,[25] and I'm only now taking my first steps away from her.[26] I've given more author readings this year than I've done drag. I want to write more books, including one I've been working on[27] for the last four years. I want to write more plays, and I don't want to be in them. I want to write for other people.

This is another spot where I become vastly uncomfortable with the temporal nature of a book: let's say *Lamp Back: Plays and Other Grievances* becomes a moderate hit in the academic theater genre, at least enough to warrant a second edition, and this preface is followed by a new one about how the other books and plays didn't pan out but *thank god clowns go hand-in-hand with apocalypses!* In this alternate timeline, my author photo looks like an antique Marcel Marceau—wrinkles, whiteface, and all.[28]

But whatever atrocities should and will transpire—be they World War III, King Donald (or Ivanka the First), Elon Musk's colonization of Mars, the sinking of all sea-level cities, complete and undying nuclear winter, or my dream projects never being written or produced—at least I'll be able to whisper lich-like, *hey, I wrote a book*, while haunting whichever unfortunate, atomic survivors make camp over my burial ground.

Herein lies nearly a decade of my work and life. This is a little bit of who I was. This is a little bit of what I did.[29] A book—like the ones my ancestors are in, but written by one of us. My own book, like the ones I read from my queer ancestors while growing up.

I can't wait to keep it next to Christopher Durang's.

—Anthony Hudson
March 2026

---

24. Trump's second presidency, and it is hell.
25. She wanted a quinceañera last year, but I had to remind her that she's white and I'm Native, and we don't need another *Merchant of Venice* on our hands.
26. On February 17, 2026, I announced Carla's retirement in Portland's alternative newsweekly *Willamette Week*—and timed it with the lunar new year, new moon, Saturn in Aries, and an eclipse, so it would really take.
27. "Working on" means occasionally telling myself I should really write that book.
28. Just kidding. We won't have books by then.
29. Put on clown makeup and complained about land acknowledgments.

~~LAND~~ ACKNOWLEDGMENTS

Anthony Hudson thanks Maria Choban, Daniel Quasar, the Dolly Pops, Matty Newton, Pepper Pepper, Joel Schatzman, David Eckard, Linda Kliewer, Monica Drake, Sarah Sentilles, the Regional Arts and Culture Council, the Risk/Reward Festival of New Performance, Jerry Tischleder, Katie Watkins, Gia Goodrich, the Hollywood Theatre, Andre Bouchard, Luan Schooler, the Native Arts and Cultures Foundation, Hana Layson, Portland Art Museum, Moses Soyer, Rob Weinert-Kendt, Clavel, the Ucross Foundation, David Harrelson, Sara Siestreem, Mack McFarland, Josh Lunden, the House of Elvira and the Reed College Department of Theatre, National Performance Network, Caldera Artists in Residence Program, the Hopkins Center for the Arts at Dartmouth, the Portland Institute for Contemporary Art, the Confederated Tribes of Grand Ronde and Siletz, and Breitbart News Network, all of which played parts in the creation of these works. And Jason, Dad and Mom, Grandma Gladys, Princess, Lucy, Olive (who contributed many unsuccessful but enthusiastic edits, when not straight-up laying on the keyboard), the inner circle, and Kate for her work, support, and for asking if I ever wanted to write a book.

Kate Bredeson offers gratitude to the Reed College Department of Theatre, Vashon Artist Residency, the Historic Sou'wester Lodge; Mary Andrus, Nicole Iroz-Elardo, Melissa Marks, Pearl Player, Matt Reynolds, and Norma Velazquez Ulloa; Marisa Plasencia and Simone Waller; the American Society for Theatre Research; David Calder, Lindsay Brandon Hunter, Michelle Liu Carriger, Jessica Del Vecchio, Jacob Gallagher-Ross, Patrick McKelvey, Noe Montez, Donovan Sherman, Aaron C. Thomas, and Miriam Felton-Dansky; my friends and families, given and chosen; Beth Cleary and Peter Rachleff, Djuna, Tenn forever; and my students for your enthusiasm over the years for Anthony and these works. Most of all, I thank Anthony for trusting me with this project and his voice.

Together we thank Megan Stielstra for her confidence and eager support from the very beginning of this project, Anne Gendler for her excellent and detailed project management, as well as her good humor and camaraderie; Wendy Weckwerth for her above-and-beyond editing expertise and meticulous eye to help our writing grow and glow, Charlie Wilcox and Jolina Kwong Caputo for administrative support, the Reed College Dean of Faculty Kathy Oleson for funding to support this project, Allie Hankins for community and conversation, and Justin Rigamonti and the Carolyn Moore Writing House—and the beautiful deer and octagons—for time and space to create this book together. In Portland, we thank our friends and arts communities who lift up us and our work.

INTRODUCTION

Kate Bredeson

I am a white woman. So, according to white liberal social cues, I should start this introduction with a land acknowledgment, as my colleagues do at theaters, presenting organizations, colleges and universities, and conferences. White liberals write land acknowledgments in their email signatures, they put them at the top of their published writing, sometimes they post them on social media with their home purchase announcements. According to this script, I should google local Tribes and sputter out a butchered list of Tribe names, some of which actually aren't from this area but somewhere else—maybe in this state or the next one over. I should talk about how we are now stewards of this land and express gratitude to the Native peoples who preceded us, and then I should receive an awkward round of applause, and then we should have a performance/event/reading with no Native people in it, and then we all move forward and forget what just happened and do nothing.

But I'm not going to do that. An edition of Anthony Hudson's work doesn't start this way.

Lamp Back: Plays and Other Grievances is a collection of performance and theater writings from the past decade by Portland, Oregon–based playwright, performer, producer, memoirist, and educator Anthony Hudson. In his drag work, Hudson performs as Carla Rossi, the "ghost of white privilege" from Lake Oswego, a wealthy whitewashed suburb on a lake outside the city. Hudson, an enrolled member of the Confederated Tribes of Grand Ronde and a descendant of the Confederated Tribes of Siletz, created Rossi in a place Alana Semuels calls "the whitest big city in America" in a state founded to be racist.[1]

Oregon is home to brutal epidemics of violence against the land's original inhabitants, including the Yontocket Massacre in 1853; the Chetco

River Massacre and Nasomah Massacre, both in 1854; the Rogue River Wars of 1855 and 1856; the Grande Ronde Massacre of 1856; and the forced removal of Native people in the Coast Range in 1857.[2] Officials established ten federal Indian boarding schools around the state.[3] Some closed a century ago (such as the Klamath Agency Boarding School, which shut down after students set it on fire in 1927).[4] Others, including the Chemawa Indian School, remain open.[5] Additional local, regional, religious, and state Indian schools operated throughout the region. At federal, state, and local institutions, unmarked graves linger; volunteers work to find them.

This is the landscape in which Hudson, who grew up near the state capital in Salem and now resides in Portland, lives and makes work. Carla Rossi is his white-faced, self-absorbed, coiffed and clueless alter ego, a woman who likes expensive exercise clothes and manicures. She is an emblem of Portland's—and Oregon's—particularly prevalent and poisonous white supremacy. Since her inception, Carla Rossi has been both a personal survival strategy for Hudson and a tactic to provoke social, cultural, and political change in and beyond arts spaces.

This book offers Hudson's sharp critique of systems of whiteness, heteronormativity, and colonization—whether carried out by those who brandish guns or those who don designer yoga pants. His writing and performance operate as a tool of recognition and complicity within Indigenous communities, and as a push toward education and deference to those outside. One of his most targeted appraisals is of land acknowledgments and those who give them. In this, he joins scholars and policymakers—including Michael C. Lambert, Elisa J. Sobo, Valerie L. Lambert, Kevin Gover, and many others—who criticize such statements as harmful when done in a manner that dismisses or neglects input from contemporary Indigenous communities. Hudson affirms the caution shared by Oregon's Legislative Commission on Indian Services:

> So, what purpose did the acknowledgment serve? At best, it offered an opportunity to educate. At worst, it is nothing more than a salve for the speaker and audience. Although it can serve as a form of apology, an apology can be seen as entirely hollow when it does nothing to make amends for the prior wrong.

> Therefore, some see a land acknowledgment, with nothing more, as a meaningless exercise that does more harm than good.[6]

These forceful evaluations of careless land acknowledgments stand in opposition to the respectful, genuine, collaborative-with-local-Tribes approach of "guesting" discussed by scholar Bethany Hughes.[7] Indeed, Hudson and others are challenging land acknowledgment practices devoid of research and recognition.

Hudson's work is part of a lineage of Native clowns who use satire and exaggeration as tools of critique. In *Field Guide: Teresa Baker + Anthony Hudson + Jessica Mehta + Eliza Naranjo Morse*, Andrea R. Hanley (Navajo) writes:

> In the 19th century, Native Americans developed new art forms that sometimes mocked and ridiculed the bad behavior of the dominant culture. Traditional Native American clowns, Koshares, and Heyoka not only provide comedic performances during ceremonies; but also serve important cultural roles by pointing out behavior that falls outside of community standards.[8]

In addition, Hudson joins contemporary artists who use drag, camp, genderfuck, and deep and cutting satire to engage in robust and sharp social and cultural critique—Cole Escola, Taylor Mac, Dynasty Handbag, and Kareem Khubchandani, among others. In Portland, Hudson shines alongside his frequent collaborator Pepper Pepper, who refutes pageant queen drag in favor of a messier mash-up of "lazy drag"—i.e., visible body hair, sometimes askew makeup, and wigs that can either present perfect Hitchcock coiffures or sit in a tangle atop the head.

Hudson has performed as Carla Rossi in a variety of incarnations in Portland, going back to The DECEPTiCONS (a performance group that also featured Pepper Pepper, Jen Hackworth, and Cabria Jones), whom I saw presented by the Risk/Reward Festival of New Performance in 2012. This loud, sweaty, queer, and chaotic language experiment marks the first time I witnessed Carla Rossi. Later, Hudson performed as Rossi in two of his own plays—*Clown Down: Failed to Mount* (2019) and *Clown Down 2: Clown out of Water* (2022), both about travails in precarious situations

(Rossi trapped under a cabinet, stuck atop an iceberg). His latest series, *Ask Dr. Carla*, is an improvised cycle of performances featuring Rossi as the therapist everyone needs and no one should see. Hudson's tools are drag, whiteface as an inversion of blackface, clowning, camp, and sincerity. Through his dazzling choice of looks, elastic movement, and irreverence alongside heartfelt critique, he embodies the *fabulous*, which scholar madison moore defines as "a queer aesthetic, an essence that allows marginalized people and social outcasts to regain their humanity and creativity." moore pinpoints the fabulous as an act of "eccentric style," a "constellation of beauty and pain, of virtuosic creativity and risk," "always an embrace of yourself when you're constantly reminded that you don't deserve to be embraced," and also "a form of protest."[9] In service of this work, Hudson and Rossi come together in a symbiosis and raging clash of oppositions.

In the performance texts printed in this book, Anthony Hudson appears both as Carla Rossi and, at other times, makeup off, as himself. *Lamp Back* (2022) begins this collection as a requisite land acknowledgment, followed by Hudson's quintet of works, which we present in chronological order: the play *Looking for Tiger Lily* (2016), solo performance *Girl with a Cigarette* (2018), soliloquy and essay *Nobody's going to fund this: a monologue in pieces* (2020), audio play *The Carlalogues* (2021), and solo performance *A Tale as Old as Time* (2023). Together they showcase the complexity of how Hudson crafts and works with his alter ego as part of his larger project, and how, when looked at together, his preoccupations, themes, and strategies shine.

His worlds inhabit a variety of venues—an art museum, a purpose-built theater, and headphones and speakers. Hudson as Rossi has performed in bars, movie theaters, college theaters, regional playhouses, and international festival stages. These works are full of possibilities for staging beyond what appears on the page, with cameras, projections, and recordings helping to shape his vision. I can imagine *The Carlalogues* as a stage work, for example; *Nobody's going to fund this* can be read as an essay or performed as a monologue; *Tiger Lily* can be a solo performance or staged with a full cast.

Hudson's worlds are colorful, teetering, and fun. He wields comedy, including hilarious and scathing jokes; taffy-like physicality; and an enthusiastic love of pop culture as his tools of resistance; in the world of Anthony Hudson, Enya, Lean Cuisine, and Joan Didion mingle alongside Lana Del Rey, Spanx, and barbiturates. Like those of Tennessee

Williams, Hudson's worlds are peripatetic, circling back to themes and references across the works. Cher, for example, abounds. Words get mistaken, identities are hidden and revealed, and there is almost always music. Carla shines amid plastic cups, plastic smiles, aggressions both macro and micro, and the Ethel Merman Baby Monitor. Behind the neon and laughter, Hudson's spaces can also be dark—as himself, he reveals cruel truths about being a working artist, brings drag to the masses, and is perceived as so dangerous that he was doxed by QAnon and continues to receive death threats. At the heart of the works is Hudson's deep investigation into race, gender, and class, a caustic takedown of white supremacy.

This collection's first work, *Lamp Back* is a 2022 monologue in which Hudson, as Rossi, introduces one of his preoccupations: sanctimonious land acknowledgment. His rebuke of this practice of the past twenty years is aimed at people who propose land acknowledgments as a bandage strategy for white supremacy, white murder of Indigenous people, and white colonization of their land. *Lamp Back* introduces Rossi—who lives "in a castle in Lake Oswego . . . it's all open concept, of course"—as a vehicle for Hudson's sharp condemnation of the land acknowledgment as it's often presented. "I see you . . . I feel your pain," Rossi says to her audience. She is, she asserts, "An Ally." Hudson's use of verbal trickery, substituting *lamp* for *land*, reflects the well-meaning but vapid and often harmful land acknowledgments Hudson rejects. In his 2022 highly improvised performance *GLOOP*, made with Pepper Pepper, Hudson-as-Rossi gives a dazzling land acknowledgment, pronouncing the word *acknowledgment* in a French accent, with an emphasis on *ment*, which means *lie*:

> I've invented a brand-new modality to help white women like me channel antiracism, and it's called the land acknowledgment. Think of it like *Poltergeist*: we're on an Indian burial ground, and this house must be clean. [*She sits on Pepper and pulls out a piece of paper.*] Please rise! Ahem. Ye Olde Spaghetti Factory would like to humbly acknowledge that we are gathered here today, in holy matrimony, on the sacred, ancestral, traditional, unceded, stolen lands of the kind, the wise, the earth-in-tune, *FernGully* meets *Avatar*-esque people known as the . . . the Ka—the Ka—of the . . . Ta?—Tilapia? No, that's not right. Um. Here, I'll paraphrase. After all, store bought is fine. Ahem: you were here, and now you're not,

> and for that we're grateful. Thank you. Now that's what's called doing the work. And now that we've acknowledged the problem, we can go back to ignoring it.

Lamp Back, the land acknowledgment for this book, takes the frequent name and fact-butchering of land acknowledgments a step further—here, Hudson begins by offering a humble lamp to his readers.

Hudson's 2016 play *Looking for Tiger Lily* similarly acknowledges a white audience when Hudson says as himself in the opening voiceover, "I'm so nervous about this show. I'm so nervous about getting it all wrong. I don't want to offend anyone. I know white people in Portland are easily offended, but this time it's less about them." Here, he turns the focus from the audience back to himself. The play features two characters—Anthony Hudson and Carla Rossi—who come together to tell the story of Hudson's experience as an Indigiqueer child growing up in Keizer, Oregon, "the methy tumor attached to our state capital," in the 1990s, watching on repeat a VHS tape of the NBC live recording of *Peter Pan*. Hudson charts his infatuation with Sondra Lee's interpretation of Tiger Lily, who is part of a fictional Indian Tribe, the "Piccaninnies," named after the racist caricature of Black children. Like all of Hudson's work, *Looking for Tiger Lily* is full of irreverence and camp, but the performance also exposes Hudson beyond Rossi. It offers a deep confrontation of his experience growing up surrounded by racist depictions of Native Americans and the effect this environment had on his health and sense of self. While it is only a partial telling of his ongoing personal story, it offers a glimpse into the origins of Carla Rossi:

> And I can't help but think of the Lost Boys and Peter and *me* when I hear those words. And Carla—*my* trickster, *my* way of mocking and wearing the whiteness I grew up with—she's my Tinkerbell.

Tiger Lily reveals the tenderness and vulnerability behind the painted white mask of Carla Rossi and gives a glimpse into Rossi as Hudson's life raft.

Girl with a Cigarette highlights another strategy: Hudson performed this 2018 solo at the Portland Art Museum in front of Moses Soyer's arresting 1968 painting of the same name. *Girl with a Cigarette* offers another encounter between Hudson and Rossi, but here the performance starts with Rossi—dressed as the woman in the painting—trying to light a cigarette like her portrait counterpart. Hudson takes over with direct address to the audience and explains his personal attachment to the painting. Here, in *Girl with a Cigarette*, an homage to 1968 and to women, the boundary between Hudson and Rossi is at its thinnest. The work is full of the late 1960s West Coast landscape and the 1968 revolutionary moment as Hudson asks questions about this portrait subject's agency: "So how does *she* feel about being a 'gift of Mr. and Mrs. Charles Muhlenberg?' . . . Would she sacrifice herself to be free from stasis? If she can't light the cigarette, would she ask to be *lit* herself, and put to an end?" Invoking Judy Garland, Sharon Tate, Marsha P. Johnson, and other "women of the era who also felt the angst of a turbulent time," Hudson/Rossi invites a fresh examination of this portrait, this woman, this political moment. It's a slim slice of solo performance that invites expansive questions and ways of seeing. *Girl with a Cigarette* offers Hudson's critique via Rossi not in a brash way, but using a quiet approach that contrasts with the character's usual strategies.

The essay-monologue *Nobody's going to fund this* is the story of heartbreak, a dirge for the death of theater in the United States. In this work, first published in *American Theatre* in 2020 during the pandemic, Hudson is purely himself. The work showcases how the United States fails artists through insufficient funding and opportunities: "What was once an artist, a human being, is now an 'elevator pitch,' . . . We live from project to project according to calendars set by national and regional grant award cycles." He tells the story of a planned production canceled at the start of the COVID-19 pandemic. (Note: I am the frowning person in the scarf he references.) But Hudson doesn't want theater to come back as it was. He is done with the routine sexual harassment, white presenters consistently enacting their racism, and the corrosive physical toll. He is done with "the show must go on." *Nobody's going to fund this* exposes the abuse contemporary artists experience in this country; it is a scream from within the halted industry for a better way forward.

No longer able to gather in a museum, a theater, or anywhere, due to the pandemic, Hudson wrote *The Carlalogues* as an audio play that was released in 2021 and accessed via an online link. In this work, Rossi gets what she's always wanted—a captive audience. She keeps them trapped inside an abandoned cabaret, abetted by her assistant, Jeffrey, who uses a cattle prod on those who try to leave. *The Carlalogues* is something of a Carla Rossi highlights reel, folding in her classics: Dino Nuggets, the Zodiac Killer, narcissism, white supremacy, land acknowledgments, and *Mamma Mia!*. Through this seeming stream-of-consciousness shitshow of Rossi holding court among hostages, Hudson offers a sizzling appraisal of transphobia, gender-reveal parties, lack of support for working artists, and whiteness. Rossi speaks of her time at an artist residency ("You just have to pay $100 to apply, and double or triple that to travel there, not to mention lodging") and bashes immigrants ("I have to protect my things!"). This audio play, she boasts, is "for my Karens . . . Justice for Karen!" She says, "That's why I'm launching the #NotAllKarens movement . . . #NotAllKarens!" Happy to have the spotlight, she waxes on about the good ol' days of Jayne Mansfield, Jackie Kennedy, and Haight-Ashbury. Sharing her own version of Joan Didion's infamous packing list, Rossi lists "2 pair glass eyes, 12 pair Spanx, 16 pair tights, to be worn at once" and "1 bag keef, 307 quaaludes, 1 stick deodorant." Her babbling flow of thoughts alongside the confined audience evokes the suffocation of the early part of the pandemic and illustrates Hudson's exasperation with failing systems.

The final work in this collection, *A Tale as Old as Time*, recounts another effect of Hudson's career as Carla Rossi. Hudson wrote this reflection in 2023 as he grappled with the fallout of a variety of sources attacking him for his work at a local drag queen storytime, an event where drag artists read books to children in libraries as a way to promote literacy and community. Following the publication of a photo of children gleefully crawling on Hudson as they together danced and sprawled on bubble wrap, he was confronted by QAnon, Breitbart News Network, and other hate groups. In *A Tale as Old as Time*, Hudson presents what happened, and then Rossi takes over to reenact the storytime, but this time as an exorcism. What begins as an outrage and a lament ends in an empowered reclamation—via a surprising encounter between Rossi and a plunger—of Hudson's body, voice, and narrative: a catharsis for this collection and for this phase of Rossi.

After nearly two glittering decades of performing as Carla Rossi, Hudson is shifting his focus from performing to writing. But I have a feeling Carla will sneak back into view when we aren't expecting her. At times, the divide between Hudson and Rossi is hazy. The themes of bold Indigeneity, the illumination of white supremacy, and a desire to teach, annihilate, and love appear in Hudson's voice and through Rossi. Beyond Rossi, Hudson has had great success with recent curatorial projects. Since 2015, at Portland's historic Hollywood Theatre, he has produced Queer Horror. Usually sold out, it's the only contemporary LGBTQIA+ horror film and drag performance series in the United States. In their book, *Queer for Fear: Horror Film and the Queer Spectator* (2023), Heather O. Petrocelli argues that "Queer Horror, like Joshua Grannell/Peaches Christ's Midnight Mass before it, creates a queer space for queer audiences to investigate and appreciate the horrors in society, politics and films safely together."[10] Queer Horror's combination of film screenings with preshow drag events carries on the vision of the San Francisco–based queen Peaches Christ, who is one of Hudson's many inspirations. Hudson always strives to honor his ancestors, Indigenous and queer.

Recent projects include Indigiqueer history exhibitions curated with Felix Furby, *My Father's Father's Sister: Our Ancestor Shimkin* (2023) and *Transgressors* (2024), at the Chachalu Tribal Museum and Cultural Center, a museum that tells the story of the Grand Ronde community. On tour in 2025 and 2026, *Transgressors* is a stirring collection of visual art, craft, video, and sound that brings together queer Indigenous artists from across Oregon and beyond, including the internationally lauded Jeffrey Gibson, with whom Hudson performed as part of the 2024 Venice Biennale. The exposition is both expansive and intimate in how it highlights the experiences and perspectives of queer Indigenous artists. It speaks in a direct complicity with Indigiqueer community members while at the same time serving as a platform to productively disrupt boundaries and reveal Two Spirit arts and histories. The exhibition specifically highlights the crucial role in culture building of people who hold Two Spirit identities. In another kind of curation, Hudson and Pepper Pepper run the annual Portland Drag Theatre Workshop as a place for drag artists in the city to develop their playwriting. As I write this introduction, Hudson is working on turning *Looking for Tiger Lily* into an expanded memoir in book form. His work is urgent, relevant, and necessary. American conservative journalist and lawyer Ann Coulter wrote in a July 6, 2025, post on the social media platform X, "We didn't kill enough Indians" in response to a photo of Professor Melanie Yazzie (Diné) advocating for Tribal sovereignty at a conference. In 2026, Carla Rossi's America reigns.

Lamp Back: Plays and Other Grievances is a record of Hudson's time as the ghost of white privilege from Lake Oswego and this decade of his public performance work. Through these plays and monologues, and the expanse of audience members he has reached—especially young people—Hudson via Rossi illuminates and filets racism, homophobia, transphobia, hypocrisy, and violence against Native people.[11] My wish is that this book brings Hudson's work to students, teachers, Indigiqueer actors and artists, and general readers, and serves as a tool of inspiration, activism, and hope when we dearly need it.

NOTES

1. "The Racist History of Portland, the Whitest City in America," *The Atlantic*, July 22, 2016, https://www.theatlantic.com/business/archive/2016/07/racist-history-portland/492035/.
2. David G. Lewis and Thomas J. Connolly, "White American Violence on Tribal Peoples on the Oregon Coast," *Oregon Historical Quarterly* 120, no. 4 (2019); William L. Lang, "Grande Ronde Massacre, 1856," https://www.oregonencyclopedia.org/articles/grande-ronde-massacre/; and Jason Younker (Coquille Nation), "Nasomah Massacre of 1854," https://www.oregonencyclopedia.org/articles/nasomah_massacre_of_1854/.
3. Kami Horton writes that while ten federal Indian boarding schools have been "officially identified," "there are many more schools unaccounted for." "Oregon Tribal Members Reveal Painful Past from Country's Boarding School Policy as Biden Issues Apology," Oregon Public Broadcasting, October 25, 2024, https://www.opb.org/article/2024/10/25/oregon-tribes-reveal-painful-past-president-biden-to-apologize-native-american-boarding-school-policy/.
4. Kami Horton, "150 Years Ago, One of Oregon's First Indian Boarding Schools Opened," Oregon Public Broadcasting, February 27, 2024, https://www.opb.org/article/2024/02/27/native-american-indigenous-klamath-boarding-schools-forced-assimilation-indian-school/.
5. Chemawa was started as one of the first Indian schools in the country and carries great significance to many contemporary Native Americans. https://my.willamette.edu/site/native-american/cis-history
6. Oregon State Legislature, Commission on Indian Services, "Land Acknowledgement Guidance," https://www.oregonlegislature.gov/cis/Pages/education.aspx.
7. "Guesting on Indigenous Land: Plimoth Plantation, Land Acknowledgement, and Decolonial Praxis," *Theatre Topics* 29, no. 1 (March 2019), https://www.jhuptheatre.org/theatre-topics/online-content/issue/volume-29-number-1-march-2019/guesting-indigenous-land-plimoth.
8. Ucross Art Gallery, Ucross Foundation (2023), 8.
9. *Fabulous: The Rise of the Beautiful Eccentric* (Yale University Press, 2018), vii, 8.
10. *Queer for Fear* (University of Wales Press, 2023), 207.
11. Kate Bredeson, quoted in Alex Barr, "Anthony Hudson/Carla Rossi Keeps Rising Higher," *Willamette Week*. December 6, 2022.

LAMP BACK

(2022)

Still from *Lamp Back*, 2022. Director of photography, Josh Lunden. Courtesy of Anthony Hudson.

Lamp Back was commissioned by Sara Siestreem and Mack McFarland as part of the Arrowhead Project at Pacific Northwest College of Art, where it has screened as a permanent video installation since 2023.

Lamp Back was shot in 4K by Josh Lunden and edited by Anthony Hudson, who appears as Carla Rossi.

Lamp Back was reedited and incorporated into Jeffrey Gibson's *POWER FULL BECAUSE WE'RE DIFFERENT* at MASS MoCA in 2024.

LAMP BACK

(2022)

Carla enters and is surprised. It is . . . unexpected. She has to think fast.

Oh
Oh this is awkward
The thing is, I got you this lamp
I think I misunderstood what you wanted

I guess the problem is if you got the other thing I would have to like, go away
Like away-away
Like far
I just want to be included, you know?
I'm inclusive
And my castle is here
I live in a castle in Lake Oswego, it's made from stone and so is my backsplash
It's all open concept, of course
It bears the Rossi crest

But sorry more importantly
I need you to know—I need everyone to know—
I support you. I see you.
Like Bill Clinton, I feel your pain.
I am here for you
—with you—
An Ally.
and while this lamp might not be what you wanted,

it's still useful. And I think worth your time
You can use it to light stuff up,
. . . maybe look for things
Or find out what the room looks like when it's dark, like at night
—in the night, in the dark*—
I mean a lamp is really useful

Oh no—you need a place to plug it in
I didn't think about that
I guess that's maybe why you want the other thing too
You know,
"land"

um
perhaps an extension cord?
a rather long one?
I don't have one—I mean, I barely have this lamp!
But I'm sure someone around here's got to have one.
Then you'd just need somewhere to plug *that* in
I'd offer my house but um
I'm out of town
Goin' to a rodeo—no, um,
to the mall
to Claire's
gonna get pierced

Listen
I know it's not the thing you wanted but

But they say the night is darkest before you turn on the lamp.

And we both know I can't just up and leave.
Am I standing on your stolen, sacred, unceded, ancestral, traditional,
past tense, land?

---

*From Shirley Jackson's *The Haunting of Hill House* (Penguin, 1959).

Yes. But I am accountable.
Decolonial.

And therefore, in return, I gratefully offer you this lamp
acknowledgment.

So.

Uh.

can you take this it's heavy

LOOKING FOR TIGER LILY

(2016)

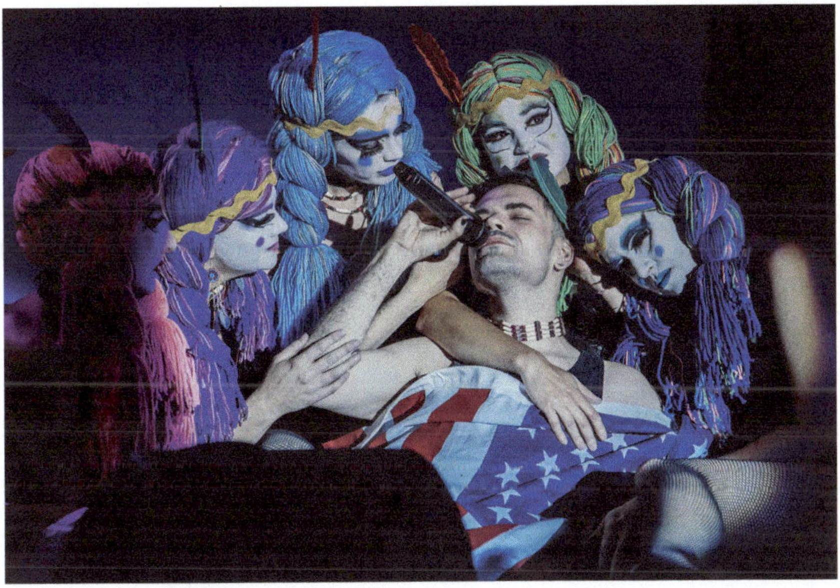

Anthony Hudson with backup dancers the Dolly Pops—who appeared as Tiger Lily-esque representations of Carla—in the 2016 premiere of *Looking for Tiger Lily*. Photograph by Gia Goodrich.

Looking for Tiger Lily was developed with support from the Regional Arts and Culture Council, Risk/Reward Festival of New Performance, the Hollywood Theatre, and Caldera Arts Center.

A twenty-minute preview of the work premiered at the ninth-annual Risk/Reward Festival of New Performance which ran from June 17 to 19, 2016, and was hosted at Artists Repertory Theatre.

Looking for Tiger Lily premiered at the Hollywood Theatre on September 30, 2016. In this version, the Dolly Pops (Rachael Camp, Nicole Fink, Allison Kramer, Pearl Stokes, Melissa Summerfield, and Lindsay Warr) performed as backup dancers painted like Carla. Maria Choban provided piano arrangements and live accompaniment. Daniel Quasar provided animation, lights, and Keynote operation. Joel Schatzman stage managed. Wilfred Barrett ran the spotlight. The Dolly Pops' makeup was by Pepper Pepper, Kel Dae, and Rin Noelle. Matt Cunningham was the technical director.

An updated solo version of *Looking for Tiger Lily* premiered at the Hopkins Center for the Arts at Dartmouth in Hanover, New Hampshire, on April 19, 2018. This is the version presented here.

LOOKING FOR TIGER LILY

(2016)

ANTHONY
CARLA ROSSI
GRANDMOTHER (video)
POCAHUNTY (video)

1

The stage is dark. The only light is from an encroaching video. Drumbeats. Then, a soundtrack to the video emerges as if from somewhere behind the wings—the voice of ANTHONY.

ANTHONY [*voiceover*]:
I'm so nervous about this show. I'm so nervous about getting it all wrong. I don't want to offend anyone. I know white people in Portland are easily offended, but this time it's less about them.

[*A beat.*]

I don't want to let down my dad. I never really learned any of our traditions. I asked him over brunch if he could help me find Native drummers for tonight's big finale and he looked suspicious and asked me why. I didn't know what to tell him. The opening is bad enough, but that song is awful. It's the last thing you want to see your Indian kid doing. And I get that drumming is sacred and it's not for play. But, at the same time, I don't. But I want to.

[*A beat.*]

I want him to be proud of me. I want to be Indian enough. I want to feel Indian at all. I want to do this show and make my family and my Tribe happy and not feel as white as a lighthouse for once, and then they'll book me at the casino and—

[*A beat.*

Then a loud sound, like metal slamming on the ground, just as:

Projection: THIS IS NOT THAT SHOW.

And then:

Projection: CHAPTER 1: I AM A SHITTY INDIAN.

The video resumes.]

ANTHONY [*voiceover*]:
You white people are not allowed to laugh at that. [*A beat*] Just kidding, you can.

CARLA [*voiceover*]:
It's funny because it's true.

[*Drums beat as the projection changes to a video of Sondra Lee as Tiger Lily in* Peter Pan. *She enters the set of the 1960 live NBC production with her band of Indians as the "Indian Dance" song plays.*

Enter CARLA ROSSI, *wearing brown paper bag regalia. The paper bags have been weathered and treated to vaguely look and feel like buckskin, the way children make Indian costumes in school. Fred Meyer logos are still visible on the bags, which are adorned with Dollar Store feathers.* CARLA *mirrors the* Peter Pan *dance, performing in unison with the video behind her. However the audience responds,* CARLA *has a blast.*]

CARLA:
Ugg-a-wugg-a-wigwam!

[*The music continues as the video footage is interrupted with*:

Projection: VOCABULARY

Projection: INDIAN: what I and my family say (you can't say it)

Projection: NATIVE AMERICAN: what we say on government forms

Projection: AMERICAN INDIAN: not to be confused with INDIAN AMERICAN

Projection: FIRST NATIONS: what Canadians say on government forms

Projection: INDIGENOUS: what we say on a grant application

The Neverland Natives scream and run off as the video ends. CARLA *screams too—and notices the audience.*]

CARLA:
Wait for it—

[*The final projection in the series shows an animated Carla face, materializing over static in the distinctive style of the openings to HBO shows and with the same rising sound effect*:

Projection: ROSSIVISION]

CARLA:
How! And how now! I'm Portland's premier drag clown, Carla Rossi—the ghost of white privilege. And that's hilarious because white privilege will never die. But before we spawn any more *Jezebel* think pieces tonight, I've been sent by the Department of Misappropriations to explain to you all that redface is as American as apple pie. In fact, I even wrote a lyrically complex ballad all about it. Would you like to hear it?

Hey, Mister DJ, put a record on! I want to dance in my wigwam.

[*A piano rendition of "Ten Little Indians" plays. As* CARLA *sings along, the projection shows a redface representation or mascot for each "Indian" in the song—from the Redskins to the Braves to the Indians to Clint Eastwood and all those guys John Wayne shot at to Daniel Day-Lewis and Johnny Depp and the* Go Go Gophers *cartoon and Lana Del Rey and so on . . .*]

[*singing*] One little, two little, three little Indians. Four little, five little, six little Indians. Seven little, eight little, nine little Indians. Plus one Indian boys.

[CARLA *takes a breath during a musical flourish between verses, then sings faster.*]

Eleven little, twelve little, thirteen little Indians. Fourteen little, fifteen little, sixteen little Indians. Seventeen little, eighteen little, nineteen little Indians, plus one Indian boys.

[CARLA *takes a faster breath during another flourish and then sings faster still.*]

Twenty-one little, twenty-two little, twenty-three little Indians. Twenty-four little, twenty-five little, twenty-six little Indians. Twenty-seven little, twenty-eight little, twenty-nine little Indians. Plus one Indian boys!

[*And again and again, and faster and faster until her count reaches fifty. She falls over on a loud last note, completely out of breath.*]

CARLA:
I can't count any higher!

[*She passes out. Lights out.*

A beat. Then, as the lights come back up, ANTHONY *is on the ground, still painted as* CARLA. ANTHONY *plucks off her eyelashes and vest. He slowly lifts off the wig with its long braids and looks at the audience.*]

ANTHONY:
Hi. My name is Anthony Hudson. But most people back home know me better as Carla Rossi, who you unfortunately just had the misfortune of meeting.

On my website I say that Carla wears whiteface as a critical inversion of blackface in order to confront white supremacy and binary heterosexism. So, in laymen's—and laywomen's and laythey's—terms, she is my way of making fun of straight white people.

I grew up in Keizer, Oregon. Most people back home know it better as the methy tumor attached to our state capital, Salem. I was a faggy little half-white city Indian in a small town, while my brothers grew up on the Rez. And for white people here tonight who didn't read Sherman Alexie before #MeToo, "Rez" is short for "reservation." And just looking at my brothers, you know that's where they came from. Long black hair, dark skin, and there they are—standing next to little whitey over here.

My mom is German—the American kind, that is—and my dad is a reformed member of the American Indian Movement. You know, those radicals that stormed Alcatraz in the seventies? Yeah! Well, he wasn't at Alcatraz, but he did beat up a bunch of white people in his time. After he had my brothers, he met my mom, he went to college, and he became a Tribal social worker fighting for Indian kids on the Rez.

So how did I wind up so different from the rest of my family? It all goes back to *Peter Pan*. Not the Disney one, no—the real *Peter Pan*, the 1960 production starring Mary Martin that aired live on NBC. Picture this: a straight man playing a gay pirate chasing after a grown lesbian playing a little boy pretending to be a beautiful operatic lady! No wonder I ended up the way I did! I blame it all on *Peter Pan*—and *Beetlejuice*.

[*A beat.*]

But that's a different tour.

[***Projection:*** *A still from* Beetlejuice *featuring Catherine O'Hara as Delia Deetz.*

Projection: *Clips and stills from* Peter Pan.

Anthony—a kid again—sits down in front of the screen to watch.]

My parents kind of let me do my own thing as a kid. I was too head-strong to discipline and I liked my stories. And I watched my tape of *Peter Pan* in the little VHS clamshell box all the time. My favorite song was "Ugg-A-Wugg," which is when Peter and Tiger Lily swear allegiance to each other as blood brothers, except they're both women. They sing about "brave noble Redskins" and it's super racist and thirty years later I still can't get that song out of my head.

Modern versions of *Peter Pan* try to make the Neverland Natives more *authentic* by casting actual Indians and bringing in Native composers to de-bigot the songs—instead of asking why—why?!—are we featuring Native Americans *at all* in a racist children's story from England, set in outer space. I'll take the 1960 version over these any day. It's fucked up, sure, but it's more like kids playing cowboys and Indians. You know, like when you made brown paper bag Indian clothes in kindergarten for Thanksgiving? [*A beat*] I wouldn't know. I had to be the pilgrim.

[***Projection:*** *Anthony, in kindergarten, dressed as a pilgrim in front of a classroom teepee.*

Anthony looks at the old photo and cringes.

Projection: *Sondra Lee as Tiger Lily.*]

This is Tiger Lily—in a feminist twist, she's the leader of the Indians. Yeah—she's the fabled "Indian Princess" that so many of us in this room allegedly descended from!

Tiger Lily is played by the very white Sondra Lee, who (fun fact!) was an acting coach on *The Last of the Mohicans* thirty years after *Peter Pan*. And, besides my grandma, who would come over and terrify me with stories of Stick Indians or evil medicine men, Tiger Lily was kind of my only Indian role model growing up. Except she looked more like the Swiss Miss girl than the Land O'Lakes butter lady.

[*A beat.*]

Kind of like me. But unlike my good friend Tiger Lily, I can prove I'm Indian, all thanks to the magic of blood quantum requirements!

[*A beat.*]

I feel we've come to a point in the show where we could really benefit from some increased visual aids. I'm gonna regret this but . . . [*Clears throat.*] Take it away, Carla!

[***Projection:*** CARLA, *resembling Mr. DNA from* Jurassic Park. ANTHONY *takes a seat while* CARLA *rambles.*]

CARLA [*on screen*]:
Hello again! Did someone order a deus ex machina? Just kidding, Anthony. You're doing great—but you could have tried some bronzer just to sell it more. You know, just like all those "Puerto Ricans" in *West Side Story.*

Now I hear many of you asking: "Say, Carla, what makes up a person?" Why, DNA, that's what!

And what makes up a Native American? Fry bread? Sure! A lifetime of poverty and invisibility? That too! But the real answer is Indian blood, certified by the Bureau of Indian Affairs, formerly overseen by the Department of War!

Tribes set their own blood quantum requirements, which determines who can enroll in which Tribe. Think of it like your blood knowing a secret handshake. How red is your blood? [CARLA *sings the last line from "What Makes the Red Man Red" from Disney's* Peter Pan.]

Now my crack team of scientists has analyzed—*Mister?*—Hudson's blood here and we've found that—

[*A jarring alarm sounds, and red lights flash all over the screen and set.*]

RED ALERT! RED ALERT! You're not half like you said in your grant! You're three-eighths! That isn't even a fraction! You're a dirty filthy lying light-skinned mudblood!

[***Projection:*** *Image of Anthony's Tribal ID.*

We hear a record scratch as the lights return to normal and Anthony runs out.]

ANTHONY:
I've got something to say!

[*Another clang or drum effect, and then:*

Projection: CHAPTER 1⅜]

According to the Confederated Tribes of Grand Ronde, I'm twenty-one sixty-fourths, or three-eighths. My dad is twenty-one thirty-seconds. Both of his parents are Indian. And because each Tribe traces lineage differently, after my dad switched our enrollment from Siletz to Grand Ronde—don't ask—he suddenly had a different blood quantum than his identical twin brother. The only thing different about them was their fingerprints. And their senses of humor.

So, there you have it: I'm three-eighths. Or one half of a half from being half. Now try explaining that to a child. And then try explaining that to a more-or-less white-looking gay kid who thinks being Indian means blond hair, blue eyes, and singing and dancing. Not fancy dancing, no. Broadway. Fosse! [*Jazz hands*] Jazz!

[*The lights dim as a giant TV with Mary Martin as Peter Pan appears behind Anthony in black-and-white.* ANTHONY *sits and remembers.*]

And not knowing any of this, at four years old I'd pop in *Peter Pan* and grab my favorite stuffed animals—hell, one of them might have even been a clown—and I'd think happy thoughts and away we'd go! Off to Neverland. Second star to the right and straight on 'til morning.

One of my favorite parts of *Peter Pan*—the line that always gets me—is when Wendy finds Peter crying in her bedroom.

"Boy, why are you crying?" she asks.

Peter's crying because he's lost his shadow, and he doesn't know how to reattach it to himself. But Peter doesn't answer Wendy's question until later, because even when we're imaginary boys played by women, we're still afraid to have feelings.

As I got older, I found myself wanting to go back and back to Never Neverland more and more. I didn't want to grow up. I wanted to stop changing into whatever it was I was becoming. I wanted—I needed—to sing horrible Indian gibberish and be as white as Sondra Lee, and I'm halfway there already, and I want to sing and dance with Peter Pan and he'll look at me just like Wendy looked at him when he lost his shadow in her bedroom, only this time he'll say to me, "Boy, why are you crying?"

[*Lights out.*]

2

[***Projection:*** CHAPTER 2: OVER THE MOUNTAIN AND THROUGH THE WOODS]

ANTHONY:
When I wasn't watching *Peter Pan*, I spent my summers with my grandmother at her beach house not far from Siletz, where most of my family's from. She sold the house years ago, but sometimes I find myself wanting to go back there—to then, to learn what I wish I knew today.

All I know is the scenery heading out to the coast sure is beautiful. It's almost enough to make you sing.

[***Projection:*** *Video of a flowing river. It is enchanted, shimmering, and blue.*

ANTHONY *sits in a canoe as it crosses the stage and sings a medley from Disney's* Pocahontas, *mashing up "Just Around the Riverbend" with "Colors of the Wind."*

He sings: "Have you ever heard the wolf cry to the blue corn moon?"

Projection: WHAT THE FUCK IS A BLUE CORN MOON?

The song transitions to an "Over the Rainbow" medley. The canoe comes to a halt and ANTHONY *gets out and looks at the screen, where he sees* GRANDMOTHER*—in the form of Grandmother Willow, the talking animated tree, from* Pocahontas.]

ANTHONY:
Grandmother!

GRANDMOTHER:
Oh, Anthony, it's so nice to see you.

ANTHONY:
My, what big branches you have!

GRANDMOTHER:
You know what they say. You pluck one even once, they grow back bigger than ever.

ANTHONY:
Grandma, can you tell me what being an Indian means?

GRANDMOTHER:
Well, on Mondays we go to the buffet.

ANTHONY:
And?

GRANDMOTHER:
Was there something else?

ANTHONY:
I'm sorry. This is embarrassing. I'm trying to figure out who I am.

GRANDMOTHER:
You're Anthony, my grandson.

ANTHONY:
I know, but I was thinking maybe you could tell me what it was like for *you* growing up? I feel like everything's so much more confusing nowadays.

GRANDMOTHER:
Oh, OK. Well, one time my brothers and sisters and I were playing on a hill, and when we came over that hill we saw big crosses with bright lightbulbs all over them.

ANTHONY:
Wow! Was it a Madonna video?

GRANDMOTHER:
No, it was a Klan meeting.

[*A discordant piano note.* ANTHONY *pauses for a second before returning to the song.*]

ANTHONY:
Oh.

GRANDMOTHER:
Are you hungry? I'm making sandwiches. We can put potato chips in them just like you like.

ANTHONY:
In a minute, sure, but I was thinking maybe you could teach me something about being Indian?

GRANDMOTHER:
OK. You see that rock over there?

ANTHONY:
Let's say yes.

GRANDMOTHER:
There is no difference between you, me, or that rock. We are all connected, grandson. We are all children of Mother Earth.

ANTHONY:
Wow.

GRANDMOTHER:
If you focus on that rock hard enough, and really feel it, you can even make it fly.

ANTHONY:
Wait, what?

GRANDMOTHER:
Focus, grandson. Move the rock.

ANTHONY:
Um, I'll try.

GRANDMOTHER:
Do or do not. There is no try.

[*"Over the Rainbow" suddenly becomes the* Star Wars *theme.*]

ANTHONY:
Grandma, I'm confused. Something's off. Where's your house? This doesn't look like the beach—

GRANDMOTHER:
That's because this is the swamp planet Dagobah, grandson.

[ANTHONY *suddenly recognizes the mirage or fantasy or dream he's fallen into—the projection glitches.*]

ANTHONY [*screaming*]:
CARLA!

[CARLA *is revealed behind the glitching Grandmother Willow image. A snippet of the Wicked Witch's musical theme from the* The Wizard of Oz *accompanies her sudden appearance.*]

CARLA:
Whaaat?! Pay no attention to the clown behind the curtain!

ANTHONY:
I'm trying to have a moment!

CARLA:
But I get so bored! Why are you even onstage? I'm the professional. Nobody even knows who you are!

ANTHONY:
Thanks for the vote of confidence.

CARLA:
You're welcome. Peace out, nerds! I'm going for more Raisinets in the lobby. Death drop—jazz!

[CARLA *vanishes and Anthony is left alone.*]

ANTHONY:
I'm sorry. I seem to have gotten lost somewhere on the way to my grandmother's house. I have an actual picture of my real grandma somewhere here— [*to the tech board operator*] Could you please bring that up for me?

[*A photo of* GRANDMOTHER *as a girl—and dressed in full regalia—appears on the screen.*]

There we go. This is my Grandma Gladys. As my dad likes to joke, she really is an Indian princess. She wasn't an American citizen when she was born. No—that didn't happen until 1924. Oh, and that thing the tree said about the Klan meeting? That actually happened to her.

She grew up in Siletz, on the coast. When my dad was born she was a dormitory matron at the Chemawa Indian School—you know, those boarding schools where they rounded up and taught us savages? When I was a kid she became a Tribal judge and the whipwoman at our powwows. And yes, we really do have powwows. It's not just what white people call an office meeting.

[***Projection:*** *Photo of smug white people at an office water cooler holding mugs and smiling.*]

So, when I started on this show, I planned to reach out to my grandma to learn from her. I had fantasies of interviewing every last family member and reading every single book and becoming the expert on Natives everywhere. And then I got in my head about it. I felt silly. I felt inauthentic, whatever that is. Not to mention that—well, at this part of the show, I used to say my grandma can't hear very well and she doesn't have the best memory anymore, but the truth is—

The truth is this is only the [ANTHONY *fills in the actual performance number*] time I've performed this since she walked on. That's what we call passing away, but maybe you figured that out. Once she was diagnosed, the dementia hit her hard and fast, and my dad had to put her into eldercare on the Rez. She would see and hear Indian kids dancing and singing traditional songs outside her window. They weren't really there. Or maybe they were and the rest of us just couldn't see them. It feels rude to chalk it up to hallucination.

She could see her mom—my Great-Grandma Maude—all over again. And my Uncle Don, my dad's identical twin brother—he died of cancer a few years ago, but one of the last times I saw her, she said he was asleep in the back of her car.

The last time I really saw her, before she went into hospice, we were celebrating her birthday. She didn't remember me most of the day. But just as I was leaving, she recognized me. She held me close to her and she gave me a big hug and a kiss and she said, "I love you so much."

She had three kids, ten grandkids, and I don't even want to know how many great- and great-great-grandchildren, and even with all that and everything else that came with ninety-six years on this earth, every time she saw me she would ask if I'm still putting on plays.

[*A beat.*]

This one's for you, Grandma.

[*Lights out.* ANTHONY *sits down again and watches another scene from* Peter Pan *before the next chapter begins.*]

3

[***Projection:*** CHAPTER 3: PRETTY LITTLE RICH GIRL]

ANTHONY:

When I was a teenager, I had no idea who I was, and I didn't know that made me just like everyone else. I weighed three hundred pounds. I was obsessed with David Bowie and *Rocky Horror* and *Hedwig and the Angry*

Inch. I started wearing makeup and layers of nail polish so stacked that my nails looked like they were playing their own game of Jenga. I started wondering if I was trans, which might have been conflated with the body dysmorphia that came with my size—oh, and it turns out losing weight doesn't change that.

Whatever I was, I didn't know the word for it.

And when I came out at fourteen it was a big drama.

My mom and I were crying on the stairs at three in the morning and she was telling me she loved me and she didn't want me to be alone all my life and it was all so *August: Osage County*, except in this version we were both competing to be Meryl Streep. She's fine now—at the time it was hard for her. But at the end of our cry-fest, she told me it was OK.

She also told me it was my responsibility to tell my father. And I was so afraid to tell him. With our country's weird brand of masculinity that I can only describe as "Kronos Knows Best" . . .

[***Projection:*** *William Blake's* Saturn and His Children.]

. . . I think we're all afraid to talk to our dads sometimes.

A day passes. Being a woman of her word with a love for drama that rivals none—other than my own—my mom comes up to me first thing in the morning and goes, "I'm sorry. I told your father!"

I was horrified. And I'm sitting in my room moping and listening to No Doubt's *Return of Saturn*—well, well, *well* before my Saturn return—when my dad knocks on the door, and he comes in, and he sits down on my bed.

"Why didn't you tell me?" he asks.

"I was afraid to."

"You shouldn't be. Us Indians are different. We don't judge gay people. They're part of the Tribe. Did you know we even have a name for them?"

I've heard plenty of names at this point. Faggot, sissy, fat-ass, freak.

"It's Two Spirit."

Two Spirit is the modern name for gender-variant people across countless Tribes. The name comes from the belief that Two Spirits are people who possess both male *and* female spirits. It all sounds so Enya-by-way-of-Squanto, and I'm feeling liberated.

Sail away, indeed!

But maybe some of you are asking, "But how does he—she?—it??—identify now? We are highly evolved hunting animals, and we need to know what he is in case we ever need to eat him!"

[***Projection:*** *Photo of hyenas staring out from behind a bush.*]

To be honest, I'm still confused. I mean, I change my pronouns as often as I google myself—nightly. I guess, if anything, my ultimate gender expression is a 10,000-year-old clown demon with an insatiable bloodlust for Taco Bell.

But sometimes, all I really want is to be a sad, pretty little white girl.

[*Cue the drag number. The lights go very dramatic as Lana Del Rey's "Young and Beautiful" comes through the speakers.* ANTHONY *slips into a nightgown and vamps through a lip sync of the first minute and twenty seconds of the song. Then* ANTHONY *ramps into a chorus from Lana's "Off to the Races," which builds into Kylie Minogue's "In My Arms."*

Projection: *The Land O'Lakes butter lady.*

Still lip-syncing, ANTHONY *kneels center stage, mimicking the pose of the Land O'Lakes butter lady.*

Projection: *The Land O'Lakes butter lady's face morphs from her own, to the Virgin Mary, to* ANTHONY, *to* CARLA.

Just as it becomes a complete spectacle, the fantasy dies—the screen goes blank, the music stops, the lights go out, and we see another Peter Pan *vignette.*]

Video Interlude: *They Called Her . . . "Pocahunty"*

GUTTURAL VOICE [*voiceover*]:
Watch out, America. The harvest moon is out, and squaw wantum firewood. She's harvesting blood for blood, eye for eye.

[*Funk music plays with Native drums and singing in background.*]

Pocahunty. The great-great-great-great-granddaughter of Pocahontas. She may not be enrolled in her Tribe due to blood quantum laws, but she's out for blood.

[*Cut to*:]

POCAHUNTY [*on the phone, holding a gun*]:
But 23andMe is a flawed system! Your samples are tested against a primarily white consumer base, so it invisibilizes Native lineage!

[*Cut to*:]

POCAHUNTY:
[*Reading a chart with her results*] Point-zero-one percent Yakut shaman? What the fuck kind of land bridge bullshit is this?

[*Cut to*:]

POCAHUNTY [*cocking her gun—which is also her peace pipe—and kicking open the door of a bathroom stall with a man in it*]:
I've come for Sacagawea's belt. And a refund.

[POCAHUNTY *blows the man away*.]

GUTTURAL VOICE:
Lock your doors. Bolt your windows. Hold onto your Pendleton blankets. Because . . . THIS SQUAW IS ON THE WARPATH TONIGHT.* *Pocahunty*, in theaters July twe—

[*The last shot melts away as if a film print is burning. Blackout.*]

4

[***Projection:*** CHAPTER 4: RED FLAGS

ANTHONY *stands before a slide of his dad as a little boy*.]

* Loretta Lynn, "Your Squaw Is on the Warpath," 1969.

ANTHONY:
My dad stole his first car when he was twelve. This happened on Guam because obviously. As a kid, he got called names all the time: Indian, drunkard, savage, heathen.

[*Each name appears as a projection as* ANTHONY *says it.*]

Growing up, he lived at an Indian school but plenty of white people still found their way in. Now he's twelve and he's trapped on Guam after his stepfather is stationed there, so he goes off on his own, wreaking havoc across the island and drinking whole bottles of vodka on a bet. He falls in with the Chamorro and he starts staying with them. He likes them. They believe in Mother Earth like he does.

At seventeen he joins the service to get away from Guam. They send him to Vietnam, and he's a war veteran by twenty-one.

At twenty-four he goes to prison, like people who start stealing cars at twelve inevitably do, and to pass the time he reads. He reads *God Is Red. Custer Died for Your Sins. Bury My Heart at Wounded Knee.* The more he reads, the more pissed off he gets. He's pissed nobody wants to be Indian and that's all he's ever been. His brothers aren't into it. His mom calls the radicals "those people." He even finds out his own grandma is white. "You know, Grandma's not Indian," his uncle tells him. It staggers him. But he has to set it aside. It can't be who he is.

At that point in time everything was red. Live red. Think red.

He wants to be with real Indians, so he moves to the reservation—to Warm Springs, where my brothers are from. And at twenty-six he makes this choker—the one I'm wearing. It's the first and only one he's ever made. The other Indians are making them and he thinks to himself, "I can do that." So he does that.

"Nowadays," my dad says, "everyone wants to be Indian, and that pisses me off." I wonder if I'm one of the guilty ones. He always knew who he was—and me? I'm a shitty Indian at best.

When I was a kid, I remember sitting in the awful orange waiting room at the Indian Health Clinic at the Chemawa Indian School, where my dad was born and raised. It's not a mile from my house and I have to go there every time I fake an illness to get out of school. I remember staring at everyone—the obesity, just like me; the poverty, way worse than ours; their skin, so much darker than mine; and those awful fluorescent lights—and I looked at my mom and I actually said to her:

"I don't want to be Indian anymore."

For my dad, growing up was the opposite. Tribes were terminated. Indians didn't exist—it was assimilate or die. And he was the only one in his family who still wanted to be one.

[*A piano version of the intro to Cher's "Half-Breed" begins.* ANTHONY *sits cross-legged in front of the audience. The lights dim and there is a general sense of quiet.*]

When you were kids, you might have called this "criss-cross applesauce." At my school we called it "Indian style."

[ANTHONY *sings "Half-Breed" as a devastating ballad. Lights slowly rise.*]

That song captured how I felt about growing up Indian. "Half-Breed" was my teenage anthem—finally someone gets me! Because nobody understands a fat, mixed-race, queer kid like an Armenian pop star covered in Bob Mackie.

[***Projection:*** *An image of teenage* ANTHONY, *overweight, awkward, and in goth drag, pops onto the screen.*

ANTHONY *falls backward with an apathetic moan. He watches one more vignette from* Peter Pan. *And then—instead of a blackout between scene changes, the lights go red.*]

5

[ANTHONY *makes eye contact with the audience as we hear a clang that accompanies the final slide.*

Projection: CHAPTER 5: THE LAST INDIAN]

ANTHONY:
And now we've finally come to the giant, orange elephant in the room!

How does a lifelong radical . . .
end up voting for . . .
Donald Trump?
And how is his gay kid supposed to react?

"I had no idea it would affect you like that," my dad said. "If I'd have known, I wouldn't have voted to begin with."

We haven't talked about it a lot, as I'm sure many of you haven't done with your families either. I spent a long time feeling betrayed, because he was my lifeline—my whole connection to being Indian. And besides—the guy spends his entire life talking about how much he hates white people, and then he goes and he votes for the worst one!

Eventually, I worked up the nerve to ask him why he did what he did—why he voted the way he did. And all he could really say was he wanted to see "change." And that's when I realized—he wants to see this world end.

When I was a kid and I first saw *Terminator 2*, I was terrified of a nuclear apocalypse. And my dad would reassure me and say, "Anthony, the second the shit hits the fan, all us Indians are gonna rise up and take back the land. Yes, sir, Indians are who you want to be with when it all goes down."

I imagined ATVs full of Indians with mounted machine guns pushing out past the Rez, explosions billowing up into the sky. And now I imagine my dad imagining *that* as he checks off Trump's name on the ballot.

Being Indian is its own kind of apocalypse.

We're the last of our kind. There's only 3 percent of us left from when Columbus first stumbled upon the continent. Blood quantum only goes so far before we're just assholes at Coachella claiming to be Cherokee. And for me, the line ends here. I'm gay. I'm poor. I'm not having a kid anytime soon. I'm one less Indian, one less bloodline. Sometimes I can't help but feel like I myself am genocide and its own conclusion.

So I make art. I follow in my ancestors' footsteps and tell stories. How I do it isn't traditional, but like my dad says, "It's traditional for me."

I don't know how to drum, or dance, or weave, or bead, but I do know how to clown.

As for my dad, his vote, as best as I can understand it—was his chance at survival, at our survival. And for me, these stories—this stupid clown—that's how I get to survive.

Some of our elders have a name for urban Indians who grow up without traditions. They call them the lost children.

And I can't help but think of the Lost Boys and Peter and *me* when I hear those words. And Carla—my trickster, my way of mocking and wearing the whiteness I grew up with—she's my Tinkerbell. Except she's a giant Tinkerbell who smokes and says *shit* a lot.*

But whether I'm lost, or the last, it doesn't change the fact that I'm one of us. And I'm grateful to tell that story.

[ANTHONY *sings Madonna's "American Life." For the infamous rap break,* ANTHONY *pops on her wig as* CARLA *takes over, rapping about "drinking a soy latte" and other capitalist indulgences.*

As ANTHONY *chimes in again to finish with the song's conclusion about living the American dream, he rips an American flag from a hiding place on the stage and places it on the ground.*

As the song ends, ANTHONY *lies down on the flag, singing the line "You are the best thing I've seen, you are not just a dream." He tucks his hands under his head like Wendy in* Peter Pan, *using Carla's wig as a pillow. Anthony falls asleep atop the flag. Lights shift.*

Projection: *Video footage from* Peter Pan *of the Darling children's nursery window opening, just moments before Peter flies in.*]

CARLA [*voiceover*]:
Boy, why are you crying?

[*A blue spotlight appears on* ANTHONY. *He sits up and contemplates the wig and the flag.*]

ANTHONY [*smiling*]:
Because I found my shadow.

---

* Inspired by a line from Robin Schiff's screenplay *Romy and Michele's High School Reunion* (1997).

[*Blackout.*

Projection: *An image of teenage* ANTHONY *with his dad, presenting the first and only buckskin drum* ANTHONY *has made. The two of them are beaming.*]

GIRL WITH A CIGARETTE

(2018)

Moses Soyer, *Girl with a Cigarette*, 1968. Oil on canvas, image: 35 9/16 in × 29 9/16 in; frame: 46 1/2 in × 40 9/16 in × 2 11/16 in. Gift of Mr. and Mrs. Charles Muhlenberg. Portland Art Museum, Portland, Oregon, 74.11.

Carla Rossi in front of Moses Soyer's *Girl with a Cigarette*, 1968. Photograph courtesy of Portland Art Museum.

Girl with a Cigarette was commissioned by the Portland Art Museum and performed there on August 16, 2018—the day of Aretha Franklin's death. It was presented as an artist talk in conversation with Moses Soyer's 1968 painting *Girl with a Cigarette*. The performance was remounted at the Portland Art Museum on June 6, 2019.

GIRL WITH A CIGARETTE

(2018)

Aretha Franklin's "I Say a Little Prayer" (1968) plays as Carla lip-syncs.

CARLA *adjusts her outfit. She sits by a painting that is her mirror image:* Girl with a Cigarette *(1968) by Moses Soyer. Fixing her hair, fixing her blouse, she sits down and pulls out a pack of American Spirits. She spends some time tapping the pack. She opens it, pulls out a smoke, and then places it back in the pack. She pulls out another and goes to light it. Her lighter doesn't work.*

She turns down the music.

Does anyone have a light? Anyone? No one?
Wrong crowd, maybe. Wrong crowd, wrong happening.
That's the problem with being painted as the "girl with a cigarette." You have one. You just never get to smoke it.

[ANTHONY *drops* CARLA *and turns off the song.*]

I'm sorry. This feels insincere.

I was asked to do this talk. And I thought, *oh my god the Art Museum, yes, absolutely!* And I had this whole thing planned. I was going to be Carla—because that's the one everyone knows—and I was going to give a monologue as this painting.

It's my favorite piece in the museum. Like, I respect—but I don't fully get—all the hype behind the *Mona Lisa*, but I totally get that feeling from this piece. And so I wanted to speak for her. All while contextualizing the world she came from.

Because all good art should come with footnotes.

In my original script, I was saying stuff like . . .

[*"Get Together" by the Youngbloods (1967) plays. Full* CARLA *for this sequence.*]

The year: 1968. The place: America.

Imagine, if you can, a "turbulent era." Racial strife. Students shot. Politicians and preachers gunned down.

A man with a black bag on his head starts shooting up San Francisco. They call him the Zodiac Killer—while a war rages in the jungle. And you can watch it all on TV!

I was preparing my Rice-A-Roni when I heard Robert Kennedy had been shot. The milkman delivered the news. They say don't shoot the messenger. In this case, I shot the milk.

Are you sure no one's got a light?

[ANTHONY, *having dropped* CARLA *again, turns off the song.*]

Moses Soyer painted her, like Carla already addressed, in 1968.

Moses Soyer was a social realist painter born in Russia in 1899. He emigrated with his family to the United States in 1912. He died in the Chelsea Hotel in 1974 while painting a choreographer.

Thanks, Wikipedia.

I just like what this plaque has to say.

"Reflective and distant, the young woman seems to capture some of the angst of a turbulent era."

I'm always entertained by museum plaques. You know what they say—

Those who can paint.

Those who can't write plaques.

And *those who can't smoke* get stuck in paintings.

[*Dionne Warwick's "Walk On By" (1963) plays.*]

I'm kind of obsessed with the era of this painting.

I smoked a lot of weed and listened to a lot of classic rock in back rooms growing up, and my dad and my uncle were in Vietnam, and I've always felt connected to the sixties. Part of it's my dad's acid stories—another part might be my tragically contemporary fondness for cults and that time the Beach Boys were hanging with the Mansons and trying to figure out how to one-up the Beatles.

And all of them were on drugs.

Just the other day I was explaining to my husband—and yes, I know, that's a strong word—that the fall of the Spirit of the Sixties and of Weimar Germany—in the Golden Twenties, which I recounted in *Carla Rossi Sings the End of the World*—are the two eras I wish I belonged to.

These times of great, forward-thinking liberalism and art and freedom and subsequent collapse. The promise before the Rise of Hitler and those burnouts under the nose of Nixon.

I sometimes think about where we are now, or even where we were with Obama, but what we didn't and we don't have—and what those eras did—is the music and the fashion. They're made of legend.

[CARLA *points to the painting, which is to say, she points to herself.*]

She's one of them.

With this painting in particular, I also can't stop thinking about something my professor Sarah Sentilles had us read in undergrad. It was W. J. T. Mitchell's *What Do Pictures Want?* and it literally asks the question "What does a picture want from us?" What is it asking for? And what do we do with that request?

I always thought it was poetic but bullshit. A picture doesn't want anything. A picture—I sound like a Minnesotan kindergarten teacher, a "pitcher"—doesn't want or need anything. Because it isn't alive. And as a matter of fact, last time I checked, painting was dead.

—My husband-boyfriend is a painter. We make that joke a lot at the house.

Regardless, or as some people deliciously say, *irregardless*—I find myself thinking about Mitchell's stoner writing all over again with this piece. Obviously, a painting doesn't want anything, but I suddenly find myself wondering what this painting might want.

Does she want to know the world around her? Does she know the world outside her?

Does she want a change of scenery? Or is she—as I said in my previous script—"sick as shit of the view"? No offense to the early modernist pieces.

[CARLA *nods—yes to offense.*]

How does she feel about being painted by a man? I think it's terrible enough that straight women have to date straight men, but imagine being painted by one.

I guess that's one comfort for her—for all this painting's angst about a turbulent era and her identity, we're just as out of the know as she is. And somehow still living through the same problems.

In a strange twist, Nazis are closer to our time than they are to hers, but all the other social-political ailments are there. Abortion, desegregation, sexual liberation, gender liberation, anti-fascism, profound ignorance, and relentless violence . . .

[CARLA, *wagging her cigarette like a joint, starts talking like a stoned uncle and tells it like it is.*]

The war isn't on your TV set like it was in the sixties, man, now the war is your TV set!

[CARLA *drops the stoner affect.*]

And how infuriating. That we just repeat these cycles over and over because that's the mark of being human.

So how does she feel about being a "gift of Mr. and Mrs. Charles Muhlenberg"?

And I doubt Charles was Mrs. Muhlenberg's real name.

[*Lesley Gore's 1963 recording of "You Don't Own Me" plays.*]

I really do feel bad she can't smoke that cigarette.

I wonder, does she feel she's at a disadvantage? That we get to come and go and know what's happening outside. Does she know what came before her, and can she dream what will come after?

Does she want to know, or will it break her?

Does she long to walk in our world, and out of the angst of a turbulent era?

Does she want to trade that angst for comfort? To be equal, and free? To be more than a housewife or a harlot or a wall hanging?

I wonder if she wants to trade us, right here and now. To take our clothes and our skin, and give us her oils, melting them straight onto our spirit with a hair dryer or however you're supposed to melt a painting onto a ghost.

Would she sacrifice herself to be free from stasis? If she can't light the cigarette, would she ask to be lit herself, and put to an end?

Is that it—? Is stasis what we're dealing with? Earlier I said I was tired of repetition—of the cycle of history—but I think my frustration also comes from stasis. That we're not moving because a bully is standing in the way of the car.

Are we just as trapped in time as she is?

Does she want to know if she gained the right to her own body—which a man painted? Does she know if women won the right to choose?

And by the way, did women win the right to choose?

Because it's forty years later and we're still waiting for a verdict.

And still on the verge of collapse and annihilation, whether nuclear or with an assault rifle.

Until then, I'll look at the *Girl with a Cigarette*, and I'll think of those women of the era who also felt the angst of a turbulent time:

Of Judy Garland, who would die one year after this painting's completion.

Of Aretha Franklin, whose "Say a Little Prayer" was released in 1968, and who died today. May she rest in power.

Of Sharon Tate, who was a year from the end, and Janis Joplin, who had two to go.

Of Marsha P. Johnson and Sylvia Rivera, who were said to throw bricks and bottles one year later at Stonewall.

Of Coretta Scott King, who was told over the phone in '68 that her husband had been shot.

Of Valerie Solanas, who shot Andy Warhol that June after men pushed her to the brink.

Of Jackie, who would finally gain her "O" that year with Aristotle Onassis.

And of Dusty Springfield—but I like to call her just Dusty—who made a name for herself singing love songs to men even though she was a lesbian. She recorded "Son of a Preacher Man" in 1968 and Dusty's star was set in stone. Like the best of us, she battled substance abuse and depression, a woman fierce in creativity and held down by an industry that fed off of her—not a woman but an object manipulated, and never asked, like this image, what it is *she* wants—and still Dusty sings sweetly to someone she can never love, just like in her recording of a song also made famous by another wonderful, doomed chanteuse—Karen Carpenter.

[*Dusty Springfield's "(They Long to Be) Close to You" (1967) plays.*

CARLA *smiles and looks at the painting as the music fades.*]

NOBODY'S GOING TO FUND THIS
a monologue in pieces

(2020)

Anthony Hudson in the Columbia River, summer 2020. Photograph by Anthony Hudson.

Nobody's going to fund this was published in *American Theatre* on October 23, 2020, edited by Rob Weinert-Kendt.

Nobody's going to fund this was recorded and released as an audio play by Artists Repertory Theatre on May 21, 2021. It was performed by Anthony Hudson—with Luan Schooler directing; Rodolfo Ortega as sound engineer, sound designer, and composer; Macarena Subiabre as line producer; and Em Gustason as assistant sound designer.

NOBODY'S GOING TO FUND THIS
a monologue in pieces

(2020)

Artists steal the world's energy . . . They become blood donors. Their life blood drips away till they're bled dry, and the people who control the world make it as inaccessible as possible by driving the artists into corners. Our only hope is to recreate ourselves as artists, or anarchists if you like, and liberate the energy for all.

—Derek Jarman's screenplay to *Jubilee* (1978)

I.

I was due to give birth the day this took hold, to a new show—a new *premiere*, that word that pops off our lips like static from a finger when we talk about the next big thing: her next big thing, his next big thing, their next big thing, *my* next big thing, because that's what art is—it's what you give, and what they take,

next,

next,

next.

We'd built the lighting, set the plot, numbered the cues, and like a good team should, we shot the shit. This was appropriate, as the show was about Valerie Solanas, who loved to "shoot the shit"—including, of course, Warhol—and who never got to tell her story, and as it would turn out, I wouldn't either; not then at least. Nor now.

The crew went to lunch, and I was running my lines (I wasn't ready for this show) when my friend at the college walked in. She fought for this work, this new *premiere*, and she was coming from a meeting (most art is meetings), and she had bad news. Something in the way she wore her scarf and frowned—

I knew exactly what she was going to say.

Within a week all the work went away.

Three days into lockdown I had the first of many Zoom calls (dear god, how could we have let "Zoom" become a verb), a board meeting where we tried to reason how to cope, how to help, what we could do. "We have to make art now!" I said. "Go digital, go virtual, bring theater home."

The movie house I work at closed. My Valerie show was postponed. Then the fifth anniversary of my ongoing series. Then the premiere of my first commissioned play. In those initial days and weeks of terror I made it my mission to keep theater alive. To persevere, to persist. To keep us entertained. To keep us occupied.

Now this new life has gone on for months and weeks and days and hours, hours in which it's perpetually six at night before another month's gone, and regret has turned to reckoning. We were so busy trying to keep it all alive that we didn't ask if it was time to pull the plug. I was too conditioned to how it had been to consider what it could be.

I knew the game, I followed the rules, I'd worked this way all day and night for ten years and I'd planned for ten more. I told myself it would pay off.

Sometimes it takes a breaking point to see the lies we've told ourselves, the punishments and penances and delusions we've created: we just have to stay the course, and things will get better.

Sometimes it takes a breaking point to see when you've been complicit with your own mistreatment. And this time, just now, everything broke.

II.

Last year I was a finalist for an arts award, a big one, one you'd call a "major award" in proper conversation, like at a dinner table with colleagues and one or two presenters or a curator you don't know.

Congratulations, the administrator said, *you're a finalist, one in five.* There was one last hoop to jump, presented as a request: Could I come to the city during a six-hour window, on a Monday mere weeks in advance, to offer a ten- to fifteen-minute presentation on my life and work?

I made myself available. Monday came and I drove to the city—hours up, hours down, hours of anticipation, preparation, doubt and breathing exercises, internalized screaming to give it all up, hours until I arrived in a glass boardroom, stationed in front of staring strangers and armed only with PowerPoint and prints.

After fifteen minutes of *Me, Myself, and I,* in which I zeroed in on everything in my work that I thought had put me under their nose—my work on ancestry, on race and sexuality, on gentrification, consumerism, gender and capitalism, drag and terrorism—I found the panelists only wanted to talk about a video I made as a gag, something silly with a filter and a quick punchline. This video took ten minutes to make, from start to finish, not like the hours before and after and up to this panel, all of it the day before I would start tech at a festival for my touring solo show's first homecoming in three years.

I tried to steer the panelists away from video work. I had brought with me over three hundred makeup wipes, each a record of a different show and a different drag face—three hundred Veronica's Veils, but of my drag clown, Carla—each riddled with dirt and debris and eyelashes and air pollution, each striving to capture a trace of the ephemeral, of the performed and commodified nature of self, and the panel glazed over.

I'd underestimated the power of a Super 8 film featuring me and my cat.

"Have you considered more videos?" they asked.

They should have considered more videos, I think—

We could have done this on Zoom.

III.

Last year I was a finalist for another award, a big one; this one national, the last one regional. The kind that makes your name desirable even when they don't like your work. 3,500 different artists applied, they whittled that down to almost 100—and from what was left, they'd only choose half.

50/50. *(Story of my life: half Native, half white, half boy, half girl, half art, half humor, half good, half bad.)*

When it came down to it, I didn't get it, and I don't begrudge that. It's a fact. It's what happened. It's how awards work, and awards are how art works. I made peace with this; I accepted it as the standard. What I begrudged, then, was that this particular lottery took a year to complete: a new application each round, and a new round each season, meaning new work samples, new questions, new answers, new expectations, all riddles of the Sphinx, now by digital submission.

After nearly a year in this process, I spent the final month—the month in which I knew award notifications were coming—in a sleep cycle marked by dreaming I had won the award, to waking up and finding there was no award, to going back to sleep, waking up again, checking my phone, seeing I had won the award, then realizing I was in a dream and waking up again, like a bad horror movie where the Final Girl wakes from one nightmare into another. My sleep cycle had merged with their grant cycle. I'd get up, go about my day, and return to bed and let it continue again. What's another nightmare after a year of them?

One morning I woke from the same fake-out dream and saw, this time in reality, the email right there in my inbox. My heart skipped a beat. This was it.

> Dear Anthony, thank you for applying . . .

I'd seen enough rejections to recognize one more. *It was an honor just to be considered*, I'd say whenever the memory came back. Every time the memory comes back.

I asked for some feedback on my application, having made it so far. The awarding organization had stated that feedback would be provided within a month, and all I had to do was request it via a broken email link. After several emails to several administrators, and more than a month later, I finally received just this sentence:

> It was noted that the project fits the format of a '90s personal identity performance and works well within the genre, but it does not further the form in complex and nuanced ways.

I forgot about all those performances I could look up to from other gay Indians growing up in the '90s. I could count them on fingers if only they happened. From them I could have learned *complexity* and *nuance*.

I started to apply again this year. I started to go back. I thought maybe this time it could be different.

IV.

Prolonged exposure to grantwriting increases the risk of turning into a sound bite. What was once an artist, a human being, is now an "elevator pitch." (You practice "elevator pitches," not artmaking, in artist seminars at booking conferences. When my friends ask what booking conferences are, I tell them, "They're like boat shows, but for people.") Your repertoire becomes an exquisite corpse of words in a document to copy and paste. I started applying for artist residencies—not to make art, but so I could write more grant applications.

Artists live in a grant economy. We live from project to project according to calendars set by national and regional grant and award cycles. Now that we don't have shows or venues or audiences anymore, we can't make work, but there are relief grants for us "independent contractors"—those ineligible for unemployment—we with inestimable income.

Relief grants have been good. Really, they're great. Most of them are a simple form, based on need:

> What is your name?
> What is your art practice?
> If you have letters confirming loss of income, upload them here.

One that really got me (I mean I laughed, I almost laughed), asked for two recent videos of full-length works. Not to evaluate need, but to evaluate product. Are you worth investing in? Can you demonstrate a return?

Do you think we'll have to write "funded in part by _____" when we pay rent?

V.

I think of that panel feedback categorizing my work as "'90s personal identity performance," and how it is used to validate or invalidate my work, depending on whichever whim best suits the presenter in question.

I performed my solo *Looking for Tiger Lily* for three years. I became tired of reliving the death of my grandmother every night onstage. The death of my uncle. The memory of coming out to my parents. The horror of my family, including my father, a one-time American Indian Movement radical, voting for Trump. Asking myself onstage, in front of an audience, who I really am. If I have a right to call myself Native, or if it's right to call myself white. After three years, was this show about me anymore? I feel like every time I sing "Half-Breed" I'm creating a crucible for white catharsis.

White people have the weirdest reaction to the show. When I've performed it for Native audiences, like at Dartmouth, or in Vancouver, British Columbia (where Native artists get funding even if they're not exploring trauma), the audience participates. They're loud and laugh a lot. They talk back and snap and affirm the stories they hear. It's a funny show, and it's funniest when it's performed for Natives.

White people, like those who watched the show clutching their festival passes when I brought it back home last year to sold-out silence, sit back and observe. They're quiet. Anthropological. Maybe one or two men will whistle at Carla, when she comes out in the beginning of the show, but they're afraid to interact with me once the makeup comes off. I want to say they're trying to be respectful, but it feels more like I have to earn their respect. And after every show, they tell me how brave I am. And it always feels like a double entendre.

When I do good, and something really resonates with their understanding of the world, they make that sound—that guttural affirmation you hear at readings and in vulnerable moments of performance—that "mm" sound. "Mm," they say, and continue to stare at me, deer in headlights, just like those panelists who couldn't see my work for what it was but what they wanted it to be.

Even still, white presenters keep booking it and expecting me to perform Indigeneity and practice gratitude for making their white organization look better. And I can't shake the feeling that I get booked because I check the "other" box while looking more like them.

(A white fundraiser once called and asked me—while I was in bed at six in the morning, and in Australia—if I could "call [my] family at the Tribe" to see if that might push a grant request with my Tribe's community fund in their favor. "Are you asking me to call in a smoke signal?" I wanted to ask. Instead I told him it doesn't work like that and tried explaining the makeup of my family across multiple Tribes, before going back to sleep.)

A few months before the pandemic, an administrator at a college wrote me and asked what touring programs I could offer. I told them I was burnt out on *Tiger Lily*, but that I have a brand-new multimedia show, a smart farce about existential dread in the face of today's world, and a lecture on camp that I'd love to bring. Days later I receive another email saying that they understand how burnt out I am with my show, but it'd work best for them if I brought it. They could engage the local Tribe on campus with it too. Can I do it within their budget?

(What's the German word for when an arts organization puts your name and face on their donor materials but won't answer your emails?)

If I'm not invited to perform Indigeneity, I'm invited to host galas, lead bingo nights, or do "fun" events for orgs in drag. I get to be the nonprofit birthday clown, the entertainment over cocktail hour before the real artists go onstage. I've received national awards and fellowships and toured internationally—but that's culturally specific work about gay stuff and Indian stuff and you'd have to find someone to do a land acknowledgment and that requires a whole different pool of funding, equity funding for anything that isn't in the normal budget, so why not book me to host the after-party instead?

Beyond the current question of will theater ever come back, and in what form—will I ever be able to make new work? Will I get another play commission that isn't about my (mixed) race? Will I get to play Valerie Solanas?

My farce—*Clown Down*, a puppet show where Carla gets crushed by a rogue Ikea cabinet—is good. It's funny. It sold out its run and the audience went nuts for it. It was the breath of fresh air I needed after four years of performing for white guilt.

Tiger Lily was covered by every single publication in Portland. *Clown Down* got one ecstatic review on a blog. Only one presenter has asked about it since.

VI.

I think of the other lies I've told myself to maintain the illusion that I was always precisely where I was supposed to be. That I wasn't gay, that I just wanted to be like the men I couldn't stop looking at. That my first boyfriend loved me, and that's why he didn't stop when I told him to. That it was only a joke when my next boyfriend would hit me. That *that* wasn't something I am only now remembering; that's how normal I wanted it to be.

Years and years and years ago I was invited to host a big dance party, and by hosting I mean getting ready at 3 or 4, checking into the venue at 7, going on at midnight, doing two numbers then working the crowd until last call at 2 A.M. (then getting home at 3 A.M. and finally going pee), and of course this is all at a bar because when you do drag, that's where you make work—in drag shows and variety shows and comedy shows and stand-up shows in gay bars and nightclubs and restaurants and sometimes even coffee shops if all the gay bars have been gentrified, because drag isn't really *art*, right, and if it is, it's *art for gay people.*

The producer of the dance party was friendly and positive and cool/queer/punk until we got to the hard part: money. I'd worked up from free shows, to paying gigs, to the usual $20 and two drink tickets. The producer called me on speakerphone with his crew of dancers and DJs and door people and formally offered the show to me—how much would I need?

Considering this was a big party where I'd seen hundred-dollar bill after hundred-dollar bill stacked into the hands of national headliners, and this time *my face* and *my name* would make up at least 70 percent of their flyer, I pushed myself to ask for more.

"For a show of this size, I'd ask for $150," I said.

He let out a laugh and roared: "Damn, bitch is expensive!"

I heard the rest laugh as I shrunk smaller.

At the same nightclub where this party was thrown, and sometimes at that very party itself, I saw promoters scream at performers until they cried after asking for their paltry pay. I saw them attacked and banned from the premises. I saw a friend drugged with a drink and thrown out by security.

Talked down to, taken advantage of, exploited, groped. Every producer, every male promoter I worked with in those days did this to us.

It's why I left the club scene to self-produce my work, it's why I pursued theater. The aggressions there are usually smaller, harder to capture. They exercise more caution. There's more money at stake.

Sometimes I feel like Nicole Kidman's therapist in *Big Little Lies*, staring back at myself with sadness and doubt. Why do we want so badly to believe our abuser will change?

VII.

I was a *drag queen* before straight people caught onto my work. Then I became a *drag performer*. Then white people caught onto my work, and I became a *performing artist*. When I was somewhere between a *drag queen* and a *drag performer*, a bunch of us got invited to a gala for an arts organization in town, in preparation for their upcoming drag ball. We got to sit at tables like the real people, one or two of us scattered at each table to provide sassy banter, a living photo booth for rich patrons. The mayor served me apple cobbler. I resisted telling him that I knew the seventeen-year-old he had dated from my hometown, who started the rival gay-straight alliance in my school district. That didn't seem like the kind of thing you say at galas. I smiled instead.

Somebody gave me a flashy LED ring to wear, the kind you'd get for donating hundreds of dollars during the evening. We were supposed to feel special. Mostly, we were felt up. Nearly every man in a tux—each of them with the same designer eyewear—goosed me as they passed, goosed me as we talked, goosed me to punctuate their sentences. They'd whisper into my ear about clown pussy and blow jobs and what they wanted to do with their auction paddles, at least until their wives or their gal pals returned with new drinks.

(Of course, whether as a *drag queen* or *drag performer* or *performing artist*, I am not a special case. This isn't me playing a tiny violin—I've tried, and it doesn't go with my hair.)

Any body that doesn't belong to a straight man or a rich gay man is public property.

One time a fan in a crowd ran up and bear-hugged me, his shoulder pressing into my Adam's apple and cutting off my windpipe and I couldn't get the words out to ask him to let me go and he held on and on and on until I pushed him off me and came up for air.

I understand Madonna's cone bra now. It's not just fashion, it's a line of defense. So now I wear my bra with hard, rolled-up socks inside. If you hug me, it's going to hurt you too.

Margot Robbie as Tonya Harding, reflecting on years of abuse:

[*Into the camera*] "You're all my attackers, too."*

VIII.

During a residency some time ago I offered a glimpse at *Tiger Lily* for the nearby community in snowy Central Oregon. My grandmother had just passed. I say "walked on" in the show, as is traditional for my family, which inspired many a "mm" from the audience. I had just reworked the section devoted to her to include this. I cried when I said goodbye to her from the stage, looking at one of the last pictures taken of the two of us together. After the show I made my exit to walk back to my cabin and collect myself. A woman from the audience followed me out.

"Yours was the best," she said, referring to the lineup presented throughout the day.

"Thank you," I said, "but we all make such different work, I don't think that's fair."

"No, yours was the best," she said again, turning her head a little as she looked at me, like she was analyzing me. The way the Terminator looks at people. The same way people look at me when they begin to recognize me outside of makeup, when my cover's blown. "You don't look Indian though."

---

* From Steven Rogers's screenplay *I, Tonya* (2017).

I laughed instinctively. I didn't tell her that sometimes I agree with this sentiment, and it has haunted me my entire life. Instead I said, "No, I do. I look like my grandma."

"No . . ." she said, dismissing it altogether, but still in thought. "Your show is very good. But I don't think it's appropriate for kids like you say, either. All the gay stuff."

"Actually, I think we go out of our way to protect children from certain content because we're the uncomfortable ones," I say. "They just see people."

"No, I don't think so," she said again. "You might want to think about that. Anyway, good job!"

She turned and made her way back to the main building, jumping into the same footprints her boots had already made in the snow.

I've never understood this interaction or how to feel about it. It might have made more sense had she been white, but she was Korean, visiting from Texas.

IX.

I spent three months performing in a back brace. I say three but it felt like six.

I did it to myself. Throwing yourself on the ground in high heels isn't the best idea when you don't stretch first. Nor is performing while wearing a back brace or taking the stage in a wheelchair—which was partially in bad taste, and also because I couldn't walk. Beyoncé had just dropped "Pretty Hurts," and I hurt too.

Six months of twice a week at the chiropractor later, I learned one of my legs is drastically short. I have to wear an insert in my shoe—not just in my heels, but in *every* shoe, for the rest of my life, so my pelvis won't dislocate. Another addition to the unfolding list of performer pains growing like my parents' medicine cabinet.

My chiropractor, unlike any producer or promoter or director or teacher, taught me how to take care of my body. I did it for a while, on and off. It came and went with my moods, the ebb and flow between mania and gigs. I started running. I ran a lot. I ran up and down stairs, up and down and back and forth, over and over—and I sweat and breathed and churned and chugged and I ran and got hoarse and breathed and grieved.

I ran until I got noticed and became a "real artist." And that meant saying yes to everything I could if I wanted to continue to be noticed, to continue being a real artist.

My trips to the chiropractor became more infrequent and eventually the doctor who healed me left the clinic. I got a new doctor, a jock specializing in sports medicine. He didn't listen to me like she did. He said the problem was my shoes. He said this after looking at them, before he even looked at me.

I didn't go back.

My foam roller is my boyfriend now. Until this I used my foam roller as a wig head. I bought it to treat myself and instead I kept a yellow-green wig on it.

Now that all my gigs have been cancelled and my career is on hold, I use it. I sit with myself. I listen to myself. I stretch. I roll it out. I breathe. I try to heal. All while hundreds of thousands die and the nation burns.

It took cataclysmic capitalist collapse to get me to stop and take care of myself. Imagine that.

X.

I'm done saying yes. I'm saying no. My god, there's no money coming in and I don't know when it will again, and I'm saying no. I'm practicing selfishness at my own expense—what I've been taught to call selfishness, but I think is just looking out for my own well-being.

I'm done being a birthday clown. Done spending more time fitting the story of my life into a character count rather than living it. Done performing gratitude just for being let in the room, checking a quota, making someone else look good. I'll offer gratitude when it's earned.

I'm done breaking myself. Done playing a role in the story of my destruction for your benefit. Done taking time away from healing the damage we wrought on my body.

Sometimes I feel hopeless, like nothing will change. That it isn't radical or selfless or vulnerable enough to hole up, heal, and endure.

But enduring is what my people do. We've self-isolated for years to be safe from you.

Presenters are still trying to book *Looking for Tiger Lily.* Through this plague. A show about the effects of genocide and me singing songs from *Pocahontas* with a cardboard canoe. An audience of less than fifty plague blankets sitting six feet away from each other, going "mm" beneath masks. In a theater, the place where people go to cough.

I'm not performing on a stage as long as it means risking my crew or my audience or my health. I'm not supporting any artist or institution that does.

Broadway is cancelled until January—no, make that May, like anything will be different then. A comedy club in town brought back its annual comedy contest this summer, as if watching amateur comedians workshop bad jokes over glorified convenience store nachos wasn't enough of a threat to public health.

I see new livestream notifications every second. I keep getting asked to do live performances, live readings, live drag queen storytimes, live distractions, and live desperation. (We're all cam girls now, except they know what they're doing.)

I'm not getting all clowned up to perform for a green dot on my computer like none of this is happening. Like everything will go back to normal and nobody died. And if they did, they died for nothing.

I hope you remember this when art comes back. I hope we all remember this instead of saying *the show must go on* like when someone was hitting us and saying they weren't.

THE CARLALOGUES
An Audio Play

(2021)

Carla Rossi photographed by Clavel in 2019.

The Carlalogues was commissioned and produced by Artists Repertory Theatre in Portland, Oregon, as part of its 2020 Mercury Project. Sections were written in residence at the Ucross Foundation and supported in part by Ucross's Native American Visual Artist Fellowship as well as a 2020 ReImagine Fund grant from the Portland Art Museum.

The Carlalogues was recorded and released as an audio play by Artists Repertory Theatre on May 21, 2021. Luan Schooler directed; Rodolfo Ortega was the sound engineer, sound designer, and composer; Macarena Subiabre served as line producer; and Em Gustason was the assistant sound designer. The cast was:

Jeffrey	Ken Yoshikawa
Carla Rossi, Cher, Chaz Bono, Joan Didion	Anthony Hudson
Audience members	Luan Schooler and the Artists Repertory Theatre community

THE CARLALOGUES
An Audio Play

(2021)

Characters

Jeffrey, Carla's nervous manservant
Carla Rossi, an immortal clown demon and self-absorbed cabaret star
Audience Members, distressed kidnapping victims tied up in the house seats
Cher, singing diva of the 1960s to today
Chaz Bono, Cher's son
Joan Didion, a writer
Voice, a robotic text-to-speech voice

Setting

The Flamingo Club, an abandoned cabaret house. It's the middle of the night sometime during the pandemic. Everything the listener hears is captured through Carla's microphone onstage. When we hear audience members screaming, they're screaming from somewhere in the house, not directly into the mic.

With the exception of the in-house chaos at the end of the play and sounds from the captive audience, all audio effects made to flesh out Carla's monologues—for example, backing songs, the radio recording with Cher—are played into the microphone from Jeffrey's tape recorder(s), which we also hear click on and off.

[*We hear a cassette tape click into a tape player. An automated, text-to-speech voice reads:*]

VOICE:
Begin audio. Recording recovered August 29, 2020. Admitted on charges of breaking and entering, kidnapping, aiding and abetting, vandalism, aggravated assault, voluntary manslaughter, and insurance fraud.

[*The cassette tape clicks again, and the audio changes.*

We hear a spotlight turn on. Maybe the rustling of people. There's definitely muffled commotion coming from an audience. Frenzied footsteps running upstairs, through a back hallway, and down to the level of the microphone capturing all the audio. The footsteps run into the house, toward the seats.

A muffled attempt at a shout is cut off by the sound of a length of duct tape being pulled and cut. We hear a chair dragging across the floor and another go with the duct tape roll. The shout attempts die down.

The footsteps run back from the house to somewhere near the stage. Off mic, we barely hear a male voice belonging to the footsteps:]

JEFFREY:
They're ready for you, Miss Carla.

[JEFFREY*'s footsteps run up stage steps, then down the boards of the stage to the mic, from which we hear a bit of feedback.* JEFFREY *catches his breath, taps on the mic a few times, and clears his throat.*]

JEFFREY:
And now, Portland's premier drag clown, Carla Rossi.

[*Silence.*]

Applaud.

[*More silence. Then an unintelligible whisper offstage from* CARLA.]

JEFFREY [*off mic*]:
Oh, right.

[*A tape-player button clicks. Applause. We hear* CARLA's *heels clomp up to the mic.*]

CARLA:
[*Aside*] Thank you, Jeffrey. [*Into the mic*] Hello, everyone.

[*We hear another button pushed on the tape player. A spoof of Sarah McLachlan's "Angel" is heard, with unintelligible words "singing" along to a melody much like the original song.* CARLA *speaks over it as it plays.*]

Lately things just haven't seemed the same.
I don't know if you've noticed.

I can't quite put my finger on it.
(Or my toe.
Or my fibula.)

It's almost like one day it was business as usual, and the next—
Gone.
All gone.
I don't know about you, but I've had to rethink my whole way of life.

How I go about my days, the people I see (and more importantly the people I don't see), the food I drink . . .

Not to mention money.

Oh, money.

[*She sniffles.*]

We don't know how it got like this.

We didn't think that *this* could actually happen, that it could go this far. That we could let it all go so wrong.

You walk down the street—or if you're me, you roll down it in one of those plastic bubbles made for *American Gladiators* and children that can't swim—and you find yourself looking at each passerby, fearfully. Analyzing their faces.

Who's safe? Who isn't? Who can be trusted?

Sometimes I feel like I'm in *Invasion of the Body Snatchers* (the 1993 version, not the 1956 or 1978 or 2007 ones), and at any moment Meg

Tilly with her giant curly hair is going to point at me and scream "AURRRRRRGGGG," triggering the horde of pod people to pour forth in a mad frenzy upon me.

It's just not safe.

It's hardly even sane.

And we don't know when it will be again.

Not since . . .

Not ever since—that week in mid-March.

The week everything changed.

The week my microwave broke.

[*She sniffles and sort of chortles, and gives herself a beat.*]

I never bought a microwave.

Nobody's ever bought a microwave. It's just something you find. You know—you'll walk down the street and—there's a microwave! It's just sitting there like the sword in the stone, and Anjelica Huston as the Lady of the Lake is egging you on, saying over and over: "Take it, Carla! Take it and rule."

I took that microwave—and boy, did I rule.

I took that microwave in and I cleaned her up, called her my own. I even named her. Martina. Martina the microwave, named for Martina Navratilova. Because she was a champion. And now, so was I.

Hot Pockets. Lean Pockets. Pizza pockets.

Bagel Bites. "When pizza's on a bagel, you can have pizza anytime."

[*Another chortle-sniff.*]

I never had kids, but anytime the frat boys next door got hungry, they'd always pop on in and say, "Hey, Carla! What's on the menu today?" And like the den mother I never was nor ever wanted to be, I'd pop a Cup-a-Soup or a Pizza Rolls in for two minutes, thirty-five seconds. And—wouldn't you know it?—two minutes and thirty-five seconds later, I'd say, "Order up, Chad!" and off the little fellow would go with that Cup-a-Soup or Pizza Rolls or Ham-'n-Cheese Hot Pocket to commit atrocities from which he'll inevitably be acquitted.

Two minutes, thirty-five seconds.

That's all it took.

And it's how fast everything changed.

And now it's all gone.

Where does one even get—where does one even procure?—a microwave?

Walmart? I don't know what that is.

Costco? I only go there for hot dogs.

Amazon Prime? They banned me after I shot down one of their delivery drones, mistaking it for a bird that shit on me. And I don't support any megalomaniac conglomerate that isn't *me*.

(I'll tell you, that Jeff Bezos, though? Shine a flashlight on that bald head—and, baby, you could light up every home in the Northern Hemisphere for free!)

I guess what I'm trying to say is—

Hold onto that Hot Pocket. That Lean Cuisine. That Hungry Man. Or Hungry Woman (it's a Hungry Man, *for her*)! Or Hungry They, if you were born after 1990.

Hold onto those—[*another chortle-sniff*]—those Dino Nuggets! [*sniff, chortle, chortle, sniff*] Hold onto them, and never let them go.

Oh god.

That's all we are. Two minutes, thirty-five seconds away . . . from the end. Oblivion. Obliteration. *Annihilation*, to quote Jennifer Jason Leigh in the hit blockbuster film.

No! No.

If we *all* work together, *all of us*, working together hard enough to get *me* out of this fix—that's what we'll be:

Two minutes and thirty-five seconds from greatness.

Thank you.

[*The song fades out. We hear recorded applause from the tape deck.*]

Thank you, thank you! That was the political portion of the show. I like to get that stuff out of the way immediately. 'S uncomfortable, you know. Oh, that reminds me, they wanted me to start by reading this. Oops.

[*We hear her rustle with a piece of paper. She clears her throat. Then, catching herself:*]

You never saw this, by the way. For legal purposes I don't know how to read. Ahem. [*Reading the piece of paper*] The Flamingo Club would like to gratefully acknowledge that we are gathered today on the traditional, unceded lands of the—name I can't say, name I can't say, name I can't say, *another* name I can't say, name I can't say, name I can't say, name I can't say, name I can't say, *one more* name I can't say, and many other names I can't say.

Land acknowledgments are actually really important, so. You're welcome.

How wonderful of you all to come out! I'm Carla Rossi, Portland's premier drag clown, the ghost of white privilege—it's not funny yet. It's funny because white privilege will never die!

[*She cracks herself up. We hear crickets instead of an audience reaction.*]

Oh, what! Did I go too far? Are you woke now because you put a black square on your Instagram? Good for you. You just solved racism in between a set of mattress ads on a data-mining platform. Congratulations.

Such times are these. That's why I'm not an influencer. I'm an influenza.

[*Someone in the audience boos.*]

Oh, boo! Boo hoo! What, too soon? [*Aside*] Jeffrey, can you check on that one? I think the duct tape is coming off.

[*We hear footsteps nervously run down from the stage, into the house, and pull a strip of duct tape off a roll. Muffled sounds of a commotion.*]

Listen: I calls it like I sees it. I'm just a maverick like that. Where's my Fox News hour?

Like I'd ever. They couldn't possibly afford me. I'm very exclusive, you know, and very discriminating . . . about what I attach my name—I'm sorry—my *brand* to.

"I've been everywhere, clown!" I've been there, done it, had it copied by Madonna, then Gaga, then called out on Jezebel and turned into a TikTok. When you've been around as long as me—which is to say somewhere between a spry nineteen years befitting an ingenue and certainly no more than the last 100,000 years of solar evolution—you become rather acquainted with the certain odd job. And I don't just mean *hand* or *blow*.

[*A bit of guitar music, or some country twang, is heard.*]

I recently returned from an artist's residency in Arizona. Sometimes to sound like a better person, I say it was in the Sudan, because in pictures the two look close enough.

Residencies are really the way to go for any serious contemporary artist. You're invited to a hosted space to create work without the distractions of home or everyday life. And these residencies really provide for you too—you just have to pay $100 to apply, and double or triple that to travel there, not to mention lodging, Travelocity fees, sales tax, plus the time it takes to set up a Kickstarter to cover that, not to mention Kickstarter's 5 percent charge, so you have to set up a GoFundMe too—but if you're lucky, all the good residencies come with continental breakfast and sometimes even drink tickets.

Anyway, I was invited to a wonderful residency in Arizona. You know, where they filmed *Return of the Jedi*, so the history there—mmm, you can just feel it. Such a rich place full of rich history and cactus.

Best of all, the residency was set up by a collective of everyday citizens, united only by the red of their hats. I guess if you wanted to, you could call them installation artists. "Environmental artists" might be kind of a stretch, because more than anything they were just real people. Little people, you know. Not like *Little People, Big World* little people, but . . . insignificant people.

Plebeians, like you! But that just made them all the more significant in my heart.

Seeing all these Joe Plumbers and Sue Scrapbookers united for a cause really inspired me. It was very empowering. It reminded me of how we all felt as a nation when we elected Barack the first time, before he instituted total socialism and revealed himself as the Beast with Seven Heads.

On residency we focused on team-building exercises. We would do trust falls and play *Never Have I Ever* and *Light as a Feather, Stiff as a*

Board and at night we would go out into the desert with flashlights and look for boogeymen, scouring the dark for telltale signs of calves the size of cantaloupes and Bad Hombre manicures. We'd spook each other around the campfire with scary stories of raping, pillaging, stealing jobs, that sort of thing.

During the day we'd drink Coors Light and listen to the rustic folk music of the modern-day bard, Meat Loaf. Scott Baio even joined us for an afternoon of monologue followed by an evening of beer pong, and then beer bong. Despite his status as a master thespian, it turned out poor Chachi couldn't hold his alcohol. Nor could his butt, no matter how long the funnel.

Fun and games aside, the focus of our combined efforts was what our curators and program administrators, Bud and Sue-Bob, called the "great work." And it *was* great. One might even say it was a divine calling.

Their dream of building something so large and collaborative—a group effort that addressed ideas of time and the vastness of landscape, cartography, and, well, the sublime—it was so powerful that the finished work really was so much more than just a chain link fence. It was a work of beauty—the way the chain link cast diamond shadows on the rocky, yellow-orange terrain and succulents beneath. The way it stretched down the horizon, reaching across the desert, into my heart . . .

And it was *great* for keeping the illegals out!

[*The guitar comes to an abrupt halt.*]

Whaaaaaat?! I'm the whitest woman this side of Lake Oswego. (It's true. I have a castle there. I time-share it with Guy Fieri.) And I have to protect my things! I don't not pay my taxes so the police can protect my things for free. Police work here is expensive, or at least $244.6 million annually for NASA-grade power armor and experimental sound cannons. And that's not even counting the lawsuits and civil rights cases—what a gas!

[*There's some commotion in the audience.*]

Oh, come on! Too soon? Too hot for TV? Well this isn't TV, it's a stage show, a *live* stage show presented in a *live* space in front of *live* people and certainly not an audiobook that you can just turn on and off at a whim, so I guess you'll have to just sit there and deal with it!

It's not like you'll be speaking to a manager any time soon. You don't have the bangs for it! Or the freedom of movement.

Of course, we hear so many calls to solidarity these days and boy, do I feel it. My heart goes out to everyone affected. My heart aches for them, for my sisters . . .

For my Karens.

We meet every Sunday on Zoom, or we did until it was safe enough to reopen—meaning nothing had changed and the death rate was at its highest. Since then we meet in the community craft room at Hobby Lobby, and *yes* we wear masks in the store—until it's time for our icebreaker game, *Suck and Blow*, that we play with vinyl wall lettering made of phrases like "Bless This Home" or "Blue Lives Matter." The winner gets to take the wall lettering back to their families, who are safely isolating at home and at school and at work and with friends at the park and the beach and the drive-through and *yes*, they stay two shopping carts' distance away!

I guess you could call what we do a support group. We call ourselves the Sharin' Karens, or the Carin' Karens—we haven't been able to settle on a name yet without a screaming match that ends in one of us calling the police. But luckily everyone's white, so this has occurred without consequence.

Many Karens today feel like they don't have a place in this world anymore. Karen E., for example—we abbreviate last names for witness protection purposes—Karen E. was innocently walking her dog in the park when it happened to her! Karen C. simply refused to pay for a cake made by a lesbian. Karen L. was minding her own business, screaming at strangers in Target. Karen F. had the "gall" to ask her neighbor whether it was *his* property he was vandalizing with sidewalk chalk. Karen X. got cybernetic enhancements and killed a bunch of teenagers in space. And all Karen H. did was drive her Range Rover home through a crowd of masked vigilantes—which, last time I checked, roads are for cars, not people! *A-doy!*

Each and every one of my friends went from being a Karen to a statistic. Just another witch hunt, another Twitter thread, another what the kids call *dox*, though I don't know what *Martens* has to do with it.

My name may be Carla, but if you replace the C with a K and the L with an E and the second A after that L (which is now an E) with an N, then I'm sure it spells something—and I for one am here to spell *justice.*

Justice for Karen! That's why I'm launching the #NotAllKarens movement.

Is empathy too strong an ask these days? When you sit down face to face and listen, I mean really *listen*, and *learn* from these Karens—well, you feel attacked. But after that subsides—well, you still feel attacked. But after *that* subsides, well—the thing is they have lots of money and are actually *really* good at amassing together and voting on time, so . . . . It's best to just go along with it, but the gel pens at brunch really lighten up what would otherwise just be a dull PTA meeting.

And today I want to ask you to think about it, like none of us have. Become an ally. Be the change—no, be the *Karen* you wish to see in the world.

#NotAllKarens!

Except 99 percent of them, who are, ironically enough, also the 1 percent.

But who's doing the math?

AUDIENCE MEMBER:

[*from the audience*] SHUT THE FUCK UP.

CARLA:

Jeffrey!

[*We hear* JEFFREY *run from the stage and then the electric sizzle of what sounds like a cattle prod, followed by the sound of gargling and silence. A beat.*]

Does anyone remember the sixties?

What a goof!

And has it been that long? I can see it all like it was only fifty or sixty years ago.

It was a simpler time, a better time. And no parallels to today whatsoever.

I don't know if you know this, but I was a celebrated author back then, which was quite the achievement considering the fact that legally I don't know how to read.

I set out to prove myself: actor, singer, muse, chanteuse, immortal demon haunting humanity throughout time, essayist. I was the original It Girl! Literally. I was doing scary clown way before Tim Curry covered his mug in Wite-Out.

Just the other day I found my first published book: *Sloughing Towards Babylon*. I had been writing an advice column for *Penthouse* as part of an intricate scheme to destroy my then-rival Dr. Joyce Brothers, when Larry sent me on assignment to Haight-Ashbury to pick up some drugs for him.

And just like that, the rest is history.

[*We hear* CARLA *flip through pages of a book to read, as music evocative of Jefferson Airplane's "Somebody to Love" begins to play.*]

I was in a blue dress that afternoon when I found myself thinking about death. The same blue dress, mind you, that I purchased at Saks Fifth Avenue when I first arrived to the city; the same blue dress that, years later, I would wear on the stand in a murder trial tracing all the way back to the afternoon in question. I sat in the passenger's seat staring at the Golden Gate Bridge and wondering what it must feel like to throw one's self off it. I don't know what drove me to meditate on such melancholy in that blue dress, but I do know this: I was a girl in a time and a place and a blue dress, and I was sharing a spliff in Jayne Mansfield's Palomino with Jackie Kennedy as we listened to the Doors.

Just between us: Jayne was experiencing trouble with Anton LaVey, the satanic high priest and carnival machine operator. They'd been on the outs for weeks. Now she was trying to patch things up and Jackie and I'd decided to tag along. Four hours later, Jayne was inside chanting *The Lesser Key of Solomon* fully nude with a man in a gorilla costume, while Jackie and I sat in the Palomino, getting high and contemplating oblivion with want of lunch.

Jackie tried placing an order for Chinese takeout from the car phone; when that failed, we prank-called Truman Capote and asked him if his refrigerator was running. Jackie loved that one, but it didn't stop the rumbling in our stomachs.

We crawled out of the Palomino in search of hamburgers from the nearest set of golden arches. It was getting late and I warned Jackie to remain cautious—the Zodiac Killer was somewhere on the loose, but back then we just called him Ted.

I lost Jackie somewhere between Alcatraz and the Ghirardelli factory. I'm unsure where exactly—the only thing that woman loved more than chocolate was an island fortress. All I know is that Jackie had vanished, either at the hands of creamy goodness or the prison industrial complex, and I had an appointment in Chinatown with Rip Taylor in three hours, so I dove further into the city—and with me, my blue dress.

Looking back at that dress now, I think of the enterprising young career girl who purchased it, fresh off the bus and desperate for a scoop. Since then, I packed this dress in accordance with a list I kept taped inside a suitcase stolen from my weed dealer, Harrison Ford. This list enabled me to pack, without thinking, for any journalistic endeavor I should embark on, or crime from which I may immediately have to flee. It included:

2 skirts
3 pair eyelashes
2 pair glass eyes
12 pair Spanx
16 pair tights, to be worn at once
1 body shaper
2 girdles
snap-front bra
1 pair hard, weaponized socks for bra
six-inch platform heels, so as to not fall over
Makeup bag with:
    bourbon
    whiskey

corn whiskey
scotch whiskey
tequila
Pall Malls
rolling papers
pipe weed
1 bag keef
307 quaaludes
1 stick deodorant
and 1 blue dress, for contemplating death

This list may be a parable, either of my life as an advice columnist and clown during this decade or of the decade itself. Or it may just be filler to reach my word count.

[*The song transitions to something a little more "Incense and Peppermints."*]

San Francisco, and Haight-Ashbury in particular, was ground zero for the counterculture that dog-eared the death rattle of the sixties. It was a time and place of radicalized, mind-expanding youths hell-bent on free love and free hot dogs. In those days, it was imperative to move through the streets swiftly, and to never accept offers of turkey legs from babysitters on acid.

As I ambled through the streets, a glimpse into Dirty Debbie's Billiard Bonanza revealed Joan Baez in a knife fight with Henry Kissinger; nearby at the Old Yellow Tavern, California Governor Ronald Reagan rode the acid waves while deep in conversation with a bowl of jelly beans, in a cruel foreshadowing of his twilight years.

Granted, it didn't help that I'd taken on a ventriloquist act of sorts by hiding under Reagan's booth and throwing my voice as the jelly beans, suggesting that he run for president on a trickle-down economic platform. Before I could go any further, Nancy Reagan crawled under the table and found me. She held out an acid tab and giggled. Nancy always had the best acid.

As she babbled incoherently I began to think about what it would feel like to throw myself from a Pan Am aer-o-plane, so her offer of hallucinogens was not without allure. Nancy, however, was wild about astrology, and I'd rather throw myself off the Transamerica Pyramid than spend the next seven hours talking about cusps and moon signs with the first lady of California, so I just said no, walked outside, and threw myself under the nearest bus. Unfortunately, they stopped and helped me on.

This wasn't public transportation like I'd first suspected. This was a rusted atrocity populated entirely by folk musicians. They looked like flower children and were predominately female. I couldn't recognize the designers they wore so I assumed they stole their homemade clothing from dead people. In this instance, hindsight would validate if not excuse my classism.

Many of them carried tambourines, while others strummed guitars or simply wafted their BO in lieu of an instrument.

"I'm Squeaky," one of them said, before asking if I'd like to try my hand at a tambourine. I assured her that her voice wasn't too high or pitchy at all, and that I couldn't find rhythm on a tambourine for the life of me.

Another hippie, named Snake, sat down and asked if I'd like to play her guitar. I refused again, but her name reminded me that I was in need of a pair of snakeskin boots before John and Michelle Phillips's house party that night, and I asked if we could stop at Macy's or Bergdorf's.

"Naw, man, we've got an appearance," barked a burnout, chiming away at a triangle. Almost immediately I realized I'd be lucky if I saw any Macy's from here out, let alone a single Bergdorf. I was already on the bus. Now I had to take the ride.

"If you've got a slide whistle, I'll try my hand at that," I said, and before I knew it there was a slide whistle in my hands and a tab of acid on my tongue.

[*We hear a downer slide whistle. The music changes again, taking on the sound of Buffalo Springfield.*]

Two hours of music became two days of music, became two years of music. I proved proficient with a tambourine in no time, not to mention a .22 caliber revolver. We toured a lot of towns, played a lot of shows, crossed paths with some celebrities, and did enough acid to put the Governor and Mrs. Reagan to shame.

By the time our adventure had reached its crest, reality was dawning on the horizon. The constant bickering with the Beatles and the Beach Boys and the occasional bloodbath took away all the fun. Couldn't we stop with the one-upmanship and satanic murders and instead spread the joy of song? Wasn't that what we were all there for? I wanted to play music, not be a lookout on Cielo Drive.

Our frontman, Charlie, may have been a genius at chord progression, but not so much at engineering a race war. That sort of thing was better handled by the American government.

So, one sunny Tuesday in mid to late 1969, I stepped off the bus forever and headed for the DA's office, where I negotiated a plea bargain and swore never to try my hand at folk music again. I turned in my tambourine and said goodbye to all that—and with it, the decade and hope and the Spirit of the Sixties herself.

Looking back now, I'm unsure what if anything I learned back in those days, but I can say this: America would never be the same, and Jackie and I never did get our hamburgers.

[*The music fades out.* CARLA *shuts the book and throws it off the stage. Someone in the audience says "ow."*]

God damn it. Jeffrey, the duct tape again.

[*We hear* JEFFREY'S *nervous footsteps running down from the stage, and some muffled commotion from the house, and a new voice.*]

AUDIENCE MEMBER:
Can you just untie us?

CARLA:
I'm sorry. What was that?

AUDIENCE MEMBER:
Can. You. Untie. Us.

CARLA:
I'm sorry. What?

AUDIENCE MEMBER:
Why are we even here? Your tape player's—

[*We hear a strip of duct tape ripped from its roll again as* CARLA *responds*:]

CARLA:
I'm sorry. I can't hear you. You're not on a mic. You've got to project. You aren't using your diaphragm. You have to use your diaphragm, like Patti LuPone. I'd use mine, you see, but I lost it under the couch.

[AUDIENCE MEMBER *musters a defeated whimper from under duct tape.* CARLA *takes an annoyed breath.*]

And now, a word from our sponsor!

[*Some kind of terrible Muzak plays irritatingly in the background. Then we hear an obnoxious, blood-curdling cry of a baby.*]

Are you tired of being held back by baby?
Desperate for a night out with the gals?
In need of a good night's sleep?
Then try Merman Monitors! The only baby monitor endorsed by the estate of Ethel Merman.

[*We hear an Ethel Merman–like voice, singing a parody of "Rose's Turn":*
Mama doesn't hear!
Mama gives no fucks!
Mama bought some weed!
Mama's gotta pee!
Mama chose poorly!
Mama's on the run!
Mama hates her life!
Mama hates baby!
Mama made some soup,
Mama's feelin' low . . .
M-Mama—
M-Mama—

Mama's gettin' high!
Mama's tranquin' out!
Mama doesn't hear!
M-Mama—
M-Mama—
Mama's gotta get stoned!]

Take that brick off the gas pedal, because Merman Monitors are here for you. Installation is as easy as one-two-three—and, best of all, Ms. Merman will sing your baby straight to sleep!

[*We hear the baby calm and go silent.*]

Shhhhhhh—

[*The song comes back with Ethel's "voice" in full force again*:
Mama doesn't hear!
Mama gives no fucks!
Mama bought some weed!
Mama's gotta pee!
Mama hates baby!
M-Mama—
M-Mama—
Mama's gettin' high!
Mama's tranquin' out!
Mama doesn't hear!
Mama gives no fucks!
The baby is immediately scream-crying louder than ever.]

Um.

[*The screaming and singing continues.*]

Merman Monitors! The only baby monitor endorsed by the estate of Ethel Merman!

From the makers of the Sylvia Plath Easy-Bake Oven.

Merman Monitors!

[*The baby continues screaming, and Ethel keeps singing.*]

Um.
Cut it!

[*The backing audio abruptly stops.*]

I'm just wild about advertisements. And babies. Not the puking or shitting or crying or feeding or burping or living—but I *love* a gender reveal, don't you?

Of course, I'm not talking about those surprise *gotcha!* reveals at the end of horror films, comedies, and political dramedies. You know the kind, that *Crying Game* sort of Oscar-winning shock transploitation. Like in *Psycho*—it's not Norman's mother. Norman *thinks* he's his mother! Or in *Dressed to Kill*—Michael Caine can't be a woman, so all women must die! See also *Soapdish*, *Sleepaway Camp*, *Ace Ventura: Pet Detective*, and *Insidious: Chapter 2*. Even *Jurassic Park*—the dinosaurs can switch sexes! [*Registering a thought.*] Huh. Now we know what J. K. Rowling's been watching. Careful, J. K. Better not wander into a public restroom with a velociraptor. [*A laugh.*] J. K. Even her name is a joke!

But alas. That's not the kind of gender reveal I can make money off of, so it's not the kind I'm at liberty to discuss. I'm talking the white bread, catastrophic-fire-starting gender reveals that are all the rage today—raging their way through protected forests, state parks, and high-income neighborhoods in climate-weary regions.

You know the concept: Ben and Bethenneye get pregnant. Yes, somehow it's always both of them do, after what must have been a wild night at Cider Fest. And next thing you know, there's an Evite to the gender reveal party right in your inbox. At the party, Ben and Bethenneye wear their best flannels and rose golds and bowler hats and strap sandals, and together they make a huge production of cutting a cake to reveal its blue or pink interior, depending on which of two Western-sanctioned fetal genital combinations the ultrasound has put embarrassingly on display.

But that's a poor man's—or blue's—gender reveal. That's right, Ben and Bethenneye, you're poor! Today you've got to go huge. If you're not screaming the sex of your unborn child to the heavens with the fury of Thor's hammer, Mjölnir, then I've a mind to call Child Protective Services.

Rick and Rhonda shot off M-80s that exploded into hot pink fireworks to announce the coming of their daughter, McKinley, and then burned down Yellowstone. Gunner and Gretchen blew up a coal mine, which shot forth plumes of blue smoke to herald their son, Maverick, before triggering an underground fire beneath all of Appalachia. Thad and Trina used an industrial magnifying glass to melt a portion of the North Pole into the Arctic Sea, and when the water level rose high enough, it triggered a chemical combination with some litmus paper that revealed the coming of their daughter, Mrgn, which is obviously spelled entirely with consonants.

As such, gender reveal parties are much more calculated and state sanctioned than commonly imagined. We're actually an entire branch of the EPA, tasked with protecting the war on climate. And it feels like only yesterday since I was appointed Clown-in-Charge. I got in thanks to a reference from Kellyanne Conway—after I fell asleep with a stogie and burned down her daughter Claudia's human dollhouse.

Being blessed to oversee the EPA's Gender Reveal Branch has been remarkably serendipitous because, believe it or not, I pioneered the *first-ever* gender reveal party eons ago. And the stuff we did back then made even Thad and Trina's look like child's play.

The year was 1912, and I had made quite the name for myself as a party planner after the Triangle Shirtwaist Factory fire. Given my notoriety, I was tasked by the Lady Mrs. Henry de Wyndemere with breaking the unfortunate news of a daughter's conception to her husband, Sir Lord de Wyndemere. Lady de Wyndemere had learned the tragic revelation of the child's sex from a parlor spiritualist, and she figured the only way to soften the blow of such sad news would be to do so with a sense of occasion. And should her husband hold her accountable, she also wanted a quick and sensible location from which to launch herself to her death. I suggested a luxury liner. And before we knew it, we were all aboard the RMS *Titanic.*

You can probably guess where this is going.

Long story short, at the turn of the century, gendered colors were historically flipped from what we know today: back then, pink signified *boy* while blue signified *girl.* This didn't change until the 1940s, when the baby boomers ruined that too. But it was my hope that the icy blue of the glacier—to which we steered too close, arguably disastrously so—would instantly evoke the coming of the girl-child. So I bribed the captain to veer just a scooch starboard into colder waters while Lady de Wyndemere delivered the big news. The glacier did the rest. Little could we know it would do so much more, and with noted aplomb.

Ultimately, it all worked out for Lady de Wyndemere. Her husband drowned and the spiritualist was arrested for grifting. She wasn't even pregnant! Together we made off in a lifeboat with Molly Brown, who it turned out wasn't unsinkable so much as intolerable. And in the process, I—yes, I—invented the gender reveal, his-slash-her-slash-itself.

Word spread like wildfire, or like a gender reveal! I collaborated with some German friends on the *Lusitania* gender reveal in 1915, announcing the sex of little Werner von Shtupp and inadvertently leading to World War I, as well as to mustard gas, which would only help facilitate so many more gender reveals to come.

I guess besides the *Titanic*—and not counting all the newer ones, for which I never receive any credit—I'd have to say my next favorite gender reveal was the *Hindenburg* in 1937. And you know, I still will never understand why the liberal media refused to play the whole radio broadcast from the event—

[CARLA *clicks on the tape player. We hear an old radio announcer's voice*:]

VOICE:
Oh, the humanity! It looks like Melvin and Marjorie are having a girl, ladies and gentlemen!

[*It clicks off. A beat.*]

CARLA:
Oh, the radio. For me, nothing quite captures the American experience like cruising down Route 66 and rocking out to some crisp FM.

[*A song evocative of Chris Isaak's "Wicked Game" begins to play, and* CARLA *adopts the sultry, dulcet tones of a late-night radio host in her studio.*]

Good evening and welcome back to another "after dark" edition of *Radio Free Rossi*. That last song to round out the hour was "Just Like Jesse James" by former television personality Cher. I don't know about you, but I prefer her hairspray commercial.

I'm your hostess with the grossest, Carla, and whether you're a lonesome lover, trucker, or just plain vagabond, I'll be keeping you company into the night and wherever she may take us.

The witching hour's at hand, and it's time to listen to the whispers on the wind. First caller, you're on the air.

[*We hear another voice coming through a phone. It's a woman who sounds curiously like a certain singing diva.*]

CHER:
Yeah, hey, I don't think it's cool you talking shit about Cher like that.

CARLA:
Uh-oh, looks like we've upset a Cher stan. What's your name, caller?

CHER:
Listen, I'm not president of her fan club or anything, I'm just, like, a concerned citizen—

CARLA:
What's your name, and where are you calling from?

CHER:
Who's asking?

CARLA:
The host of the show you're calling.

CHER:
Oh right. Um. My name is—um, Rusty. No, Tess. Um.

CARLA:
Rusty Tessum?

CHER:
Yeah, but the gals downtown call me "Mamma Mia" for short.

CARLA:
Mamma Mia?

CHER:
Yeah, it's—Italian.

CARLA:
I think "Mamma Mia" is more of a phrase, or an Alka-Seltzer commercial, or a musica—

CHER:
Schenectady!

CARLA:
What?

CHER:
You asked where I'm from, I'm from Schenec—tady.

CARLA:
Rusty "Mamma Mia" Tessum from Schenectady, everyone—

CHER:
Hi yeah thanks OK great being on. Now back to your bullying of Cher—

CARLA:
It was a joke about a hairspray commercial.

CHER:
It was a hairspray infomercial, and I'll have you know I'm—Cher is an enterprising business woman, and she's had to fight to survive, you know.

CARLA:
It's rough for an aging woman in Hollywood.

CHER:
Who the fuck are you calling aging?

CARLA:
Whoa whoa whoa! Language. This isn't the Howard Stern show!

CHER:
Yeah, well if I was the MPAA or whatever I'd fine your ass for crimes against Cher—

CARLA:
I think you mean the FCC?

CHER:
FCC-U-K.

CARLA:
Oh, I see what you did there. You sound like a Cher tweet.

CHER:
I have dyslexia—I mean Cher has dyslexia. That's not funny.

CARLA:
No, absolutely not—

CHER:
I'd like to see you work half as hard as she does! She's a two-time Academy Award winner you know.

CARLA:
She only won one Academy Award, for *Moonstruck*—

CHER:
Don't you think I know that? What I meant was two-time nominee, one-time winner, though she sure as shit shoulda won for *Silkwood*. Only reason I didn't was because everyone was too busy watching Kurt Russell's goddamn pillow lips.

CARLA:
Only reason you didn't win?

CHER:
—you didn't let me finish—is what I said to the Academy in my letter to them disagreeing with their choice. I'm an Academy member, you see.

CARLA:
Rusty Tessum is a member of the Academy of Motion Picture Arts and Sciences? What do you do for a living, Rusty?

CHER:
I . . . run a barbeque shack.

CARLA:
But you belong to the Academy?

CHER:
Yeah, I . . . I teach film out the back.

CARLA:
Such a multifaceted life.

CHER:
Multifaceted! That's the word I put in my typed letter to the Academy. In defense of Cher. She's multifaceted. She's an Oscar nominee, Oscar winner, Emmy nominee, Emmy winner, Grammy nominee, Grammy winner, Tony nominee . . . uh—

CARLA:
Not an EGOT but an EGO!

CHER:
Who you saying's got an ego?

CARLA:
It's an acronym, but—

CHER:
You're an acronymph! Listen, I really don't like the way you talk about Cher—

[*We hear a muffled male voice in the background of the woman's phone line. We hear her speak away from the telephone*:]

Mommy's making an important call. To Ryan Murphy. Yeah, I'm trying to get you back on *American Horror Story*, sweet cheeks. Fingers crossed. Go back to bed.

[*She returns to the phone*:]

Anyway, where was I?

CARLA:
You were pretending you aren't Cher.

CHER:
[*She scoffs with feigned speechlessness once, twice, three times.*] Wow! Wow, you know what? I don't run a barbeque shack and teach film here in Schenectaville just to be treated like this, and you know what, neither does Cher!

[*She hangs up. We hear a loud dial tone before it cuts or fades out.*]

CARLA:
OK. "Rusty Tessum" from "Schenectaville," everyone. You can't win 'em all over.

But how are the rest of you? In the next block we'll have "Nine from the '90s." But right now I want to hear from you—because these nights are lovely, dark, and deep, and we've got miles to go before we sleep. That's miles to go before *you* sleep.* Next caller, you're on the air.

* From Quentin Tarantino's screenplay *Death Proof* (2007), which echoes lines in Robert Frost's poem "Stopping by Woods on a Snowy Evening" (1923).

CHER:
Hey, bitch.

CARLA:
Oh, look, it's "Rusty" again.

CHER:
No, my name's . . . Zed.

CARLA:
Oh? Scuse me. Zed.

CHER:
Yeah. I'm a police—man. And you're under arrest.

CARLA:
Over the air?

CHER:
For crimes. Against Cher.

CARLA:
I didn't know there was such a thing.

CHER:
I'm with the radio crimes division. It's like the vice squad but for soft FM.

CARLA:
And you're calling in an arrest.

CHER:
You have the right to shut the fuck up.

CARLA:
OK, OK, OK, once again—

[*We hear someone pick up a second phone line on the open line and try dialing a phone number. Then we clearly hear the more muffled voice from before.*]

CHAZ:
Hi, I'd like to order a cheese pizza.

CHER:
Chaz, Mommy's on the phone.

CARLA:
I'm sorry, what's happening?

CHAZ:
Quit hogging the line!

CHER:
Mommy will heat you up some Swift Premium Brown 'N Serve when she's done.

CHAZ:
But, Moooom, I'm hungry *now!*

CHER:
I know, sweetheart, but—

CARLA:
Zed, sounds like you've got some more arrests to make!

CHAZ:
Who's arresting me?

CHER:
Nobody, sweetheart.

CHAZ:
Who's Zed?

CHER:
Zed's dead, baby, Zed's dead.*

* From Tarantino's screenplay *Pulp Fiction* (1994).

CARLA:
I thought you were Officer Zed?

CHER:
Yeah um, I am, I . . . I'm like *Ghost Dad*, but I'm a cop.

CHAZ:
[*Sincere*] I thought you were my mom, Academy Award nominee Cher.

CHER:
Academy Award *winner*! And, Chaz, Mommy—Officer Zed—needs you to hang up the phone in the name of the law, sweetheart.

CHAZ:
OK, Officer Zed, and then cheese pizza?

CHER:
Pizza isn't gonna happen, it's Swift Premium Brown 'N Serve.

CHAZ:
[*Dragging*] O-K.

[CHAZ *hangs up.*]

CARLA:
Must be busy down at the station.

CHER:
Let me tell ya, the inmates sure are unruly tonight!

CARLA:
Sounds like it.

CHER:
Bet it's got you *scared straight*, huh? Thinking some second thoughts about running that mouth of yours?

CARLA:
Oh, you know it. Boy, have I learned my lesson.

CHER:
Good. Now you keep your lips zipped on all matters *Cher*, and I won't have to take you downtown.

CARLA:
Yes, Officer Zed.

CHER:
OK. Um. Roger roger. Over and out, citizen.

[*She hangs up and the dial tone fades out again. After a beat.*]

CARLA:
I don't know about you, but I for one can't wait to see *Mamma Mia!: Tokyo Drift*, especially now that we know Cher's got nothing else to do with her time . . .

But that's another story for another clown. I want to hear from my nighttime wanderers and soulful travelers here on *Radio Free Rossi*—after dark! How's our time together treating you? Next caller, you're on the air.

CHER:
YOU KNOW WHAT? FUCK YOU—YOU PIECE OF SH—

[*The entire sequence is replaced with a loud dial tone. After a good fade,* CARLA *returns.*]

CARLA:
Suffice to say, *Radio Free Rossi* was short-lived. After another on-air incident with Kanye Kardashian, they gave my slot to—shiver—Joe Rogan.

Oh well. It's a dying medium anyway.

[*A beat. An audience member says something muffled.*]

AUDIENCE MEMBER:
Mmmf!

[*Carla ignores them.*]

CARLA:
Anyone know what time it is?

Oh, right. You're tied up.

[*A beat*] Um.

Well, this is awkward.

I forgot the rest of the show.

So.

Uh.

Sure could use some filler—

[*A beat*] What's that line . . . what's that line?

Something something. What's the—something something. What's that—something something something. Something two—two oysters, no, two clams—no, two, oy—two clams, no, oysters, no, cla—two oysters, no clams, no, two cla—two oysters walk into a bar! *Aw shucks*, they said.

Haaa!

That's a knee-slapper.

[*To the audience, said with a frowny face*] Oh, you can't do that either.

[*Off the mic*] Jeffrey, keep an eye and make sure they can't do that either.

[*There is some muffled commotion in the audience.*]

[*A beat*] Jeffrey, can they do that either? Because it sounds like they can do that either.

[*We hear an audience member's chair tip over, and they begin screaming for help as loud as they can from under duct tape.*]

AUDIENCE MEMBER:
HLF HLF HLLLLLLLFF!!!!

CARLA:
Jeffrey! They can do that either!

[*We hear* JEFFREY*'s frenzied footsteps in the house.*]

JEFFREY:
Apologies, Miss Carla!

[*We hear him kick the audience member's chair.*]

AUDIENCE MEMBER:
MMMF!

JEFFREY:
[*Off mic*] Don't make me send you to the cornfields.

AUDIENCE MEMBER:
Mmmfgn-mmm?

CARLA:
I'm sorry. I should explain. Jeffrey spends his days in a pantry watching episodes of *The Twilight Zone* on loop. I've been learning about French parenting.

AUDIENCE MEMBER:
MFMFMMMNGRG!

CARLA:
Jeffrey, clean up on aisle—*NOW*!

JEFFREY:
Yes, Miss Carla.

[*We hear* JEFFREY *lift and lean the chair—and the muffled audience member—on its back legs before he drags it out of the room.*]

CARLA:
This is probably a good time to remind you to silence your cell phones. [*She directs her words to* JEFFREY, *off mic, as he shuts a loud door to the house.*] Thank you, Jeffrey.

Now where was I? Not oysters . . . oh yes, that was it!

Lately I find myself—

[*She is interrupted by the sound of an extremely heavy, bludgeon-like impact beyond the door* JEFFREY *has shut. Even muffled, we hear the resulting unintelligible exclamation of the audience member behind the door.* CARLA *gives it a second.*]

Lately I find myself—

[*We hear another bludgeon and another exclamation. She gives it another second.*]

Lately I find myself—

[*Another bludgeon, another exclamation, another second.*]

Lately I find myself—

[CARLA *stops herself this time. She listens for a beat. We hear the door slowly creak open and* JEFFREY*'s footsteps.*]

[*slightly off mic*] Everything kosher, Jeffrey?

JEFFREY [*off mic*]:
Yes, Miss Carla.

CARLA [*slightly off mic*]:
Good. You may help yourself to another Ring Pop.

[*A beat*] Lately I find myself looking back to the olden days—wistfully, like a college lesbian staring down a sorority hallway. You know, back when America was great, the first time?

Stable temperatures. Smoking on airplanes. Presidents who got stuck in bathtubs instead of the toilet and Twitter.

My salad days.

And school days!

Getting by with a little help from your friends—on the college green, with some college grass.

I was never a student, of course. Ha! As if that wasn't obvious. You couldn't find someone more unqualified. No, I was a professor.

I know what you're thinking—turning tricks comes with better pay and benefits than adjunct work, and you don't have to turn in your knife at the front desk. This is all true. But I do miss the sense of collaboration and community.

The sharing of knowledge. Peer reviews. Words like *onus*, which sounds like *anus*. The armed campus police and the occasional Christmas card from Betsy DeVos. And let me tell you, that woman fuckin' crushes it at beer pong like no other.

[*We hear a large cart of some sort as it is rolled out onto the stage, followed by the sound of a projection screen getting pulled down.*]

With the pandemic, it seems school's out for summer, and it's looking to be a long summer at that. An Indian sum—I'm sorry, a *Native American* summer.

But now, in these days of Zoom, are we not all students at Trump U?

[*We hear a slide projector whir to life. The tape player clicks and Saint-Saëns's "Danse Macabre" is heard. Throughout* CARLA's *lecture we hear slides change.*]

I'd like to thank my fellow fellows for attending this lecture tonight at the Institute for Metaphysical and Digestive Clown Research, as presented by I, Dr. Carla Rossi, Professor Emeritus of Butt Studies, PhD, DP, DVDA.

Tonight's lecture takes us all the way back to the beginning—I think you'll agree, a very good place to start—in A.D. 1500. I think you'll also agree, not a very good time to be alive.

The Black Death had been vanquished only one hundred years before, and the Renaissance was just beginning to take hold, not unlike when you remember to turn on air conditioning midway through the car ride.

Our central character is one Hieronymus Bosch, the Dutch painter as well known for his grotesque and fantastical paintings as for his subtly noodle-like hair. And his preferred subject matter was the unmitigated, undulating corpulence of the reproductive masses, also known as "Discount Tuesday" at the corporate Cineplex. As you'll see, the horrors of modernity are remarkably like those of the Middle Ages.

My primary focus tonight is *The Garden of Earthly Delights*, Bosch's magnum opus, meaning an opus that is not only larger than most, but also ribbed for her pleasure.

The Garden of Earthly Delights is a triptych, or three-part painting, which is also sometimes called a threesome by more adventurous, liberal-minded scholars.

On the left panel of the painting you can see Adam and Eve in the Garden of Eden.

[*Carla clicks a button to bring up a slide of the panel. The projector jams and whirs.*]

On the left panel you can see—

[*She clicks, and it jams again.*]

Oh, goddamnit. Jeffrey, the slide projector is jammed.

[*We hear his footsteps.*]

JEFFREY [*off mic, sincere*]:
Did you try taking out the slide and blowing on it?

CARLA:
How very dare you.

JEFFREY:
My apologies, Miss Carla.

[*She tries clicking it again, and it overheats and dies.*]

CARLA:
The person I stole this from paid good money for it. It worked perfectly well thirty years ago. Oh well.

[*We hear her chuck the projector remote, which hits another muffled audience member.*]

AUDIENCE MEMBER:
MFFFM!

CARLA:
As I was saying. The left panel depicts Adam and Eve in the Garden of Eden, exactly as we remember the story: pasty, lithe, nude—just another pair of twinks in a Czechoslovakian porno.

The middle panel of the painting is best described as a crustacean Disneyland gone wrong. Eve's sin has turned the garden into an orgy, a bacchanal, a HomeTown Buffet with heaping sides of sex gravy.

And finally, the far-right panel treats us to the punishing fires of Hell. Pigs dress as nuns, giant birds devour human beings whole. Ducks are transmuted into waterslides and knives explode out of ears that look like butts. Withering souls are lashed and impaled while a dinner party finds itself seated within a giant prolapse—just another night at Mar-a-Lago.

But what I find most fascinating about this panel is a tableau placed just below its midpoint: Bosch has painted a pair of legs stemming from a pair of buttocks and inscribed with music notes.

On the butt.

Butt, of course, from the Latin *clunis*, which roughly translates today to *doodymaker*.

How curious!

Bosch's butt melody—as seen here—has long been viewed by academia as the equivalent of a non sequitur or, at best, a stoner joke, not unlike the music of Florence Foster Jenkins or the complete works of J. K. Rowling.

It wasn't until the middle of last year that an enterprising composer known simply as YouTube user XTina6969 entered the painted musical notes into a computer program and generated the first-ever recording of Bosch's butt song. The following is what XTina6969—and what Bosch five hundred years ago—presented to the world.

[*We hear the tape player cue up and play the song in its entirety.*]

As the cheeriness of the song suggests, the Middle Ages really were quite shit.

Flash forward—and yet still ever back in time—to another revolutionary butt song that continued to pave the way for this underrepresented genre.

In 1934, after the success of "On the Good Ship Lollipop," studio execs wanted to try a more in-your-face edge with Shirley Temple's next single. Thus came Shirley's one-time foray into *proto rap* with the anthem "Toot Toot Goes My Brown Flute." Unfortunately, no recordings survive, but pop culture archaeologists have excavated the following fragmentary lyrics:

Toot toot
Goes my brown flute
Tooted so fast I soiled my boot
Watch out, daddy
Better line that zoot suit

Despite the resulting controversy, which only subsided thanks to the Lindbergh baby trial, Shirley's early—one might even say "primitive"—foray into butt music paved the way for Sir Mix-a-Lot and his eponymous "Baby Got Back," Sisqó's "Thong Song," Nicki Minaj's "Anaconda," and more recently, the quintessential anthem of our time, Samwell's "What What (In the Butt)."

If anything, the success of these butt songs suggests that all Bosch was lacking in his composition were provocative lyrics with killer dance moves, and an ample dose of gyration.

But today I am ecstatic to announce that after years of tireless research, I have at long last discovered the lyrics our Dutch painter intended to pair with his infamous butt song! A complex cam-er-a powerful enough to zoom into the collective unconscious has made these lyrics accessible, through a new scientific process much like what was featured in Christopher Nolan's blockbuster film *Inception*, except it makes sense.

[*Slightly off mic*] Jeffrey, can you please bring me the lyrics? The ones in the sealed envelope.

[*We hear some steps and a paper handoff.*]

Oh my word. Fresh from computer analysis. Well—here we go.

[*We hear her rip open the envelope.*]

My friends, behold. For the first time ever heard by human ears, I give you Hieronymous Bosch's "Music of the Butt."

[*The tape player plays the song one more time, and* CARLA *sings along, discovering the lyrics as she goes.*]

Butt butt butt butt butt butt butt
Butt butt butt butt butt butt butt
Ouch my
Butt butt butt butt butt butt butt butt
It burns—ow!—please help my butt
Please could you get me some Pep-to-Bis-mol
O my god—ow!—it really burns

[*The song ends. There is silence.* CARLA *is stunned. An audience member coughs.*]

CARLA:
[*Crushed*] After all these years, the butt song has been revealed as the first-ever commercial jingle.

After spending my entire professional life and countless tax dollars not belonging to me, it seems I have no choice but to come to terms with this life-crushing disappointment. For, as Ayn Rand wrote before someone pointed out that nobody cares, "Life is pain."

[*A beat.*]

[*Dead inside*] Ha.

In closing, I should like to send us off with a poetic meditation I feel captures not only the elusive qualities of the posterior and its infernal melodies, but also the meaninglessness of existence and all its scatological shortcomings. The following is drawn from the concluding stanza of Emily Dickinson's final poem, and I shall do my utmost to serve the master's words justly.

[*She clears her throat.*]

We step like Plush,
We stand like snow,
The waters murmur new,
Three rivers and the Hill are passed—
Two deserts and the sea!
Now Death usurps my Premium
And sneaks a peek at my Boo-ty.

[*A beat.*]

Thank you, and goodnight.

[*Silence.* CARLA *clears her throat very expectantly.*]

CARLA:
A-HEM!

[*We hear the sound of one audience member sadly trying to clap their hands while bound.*]

Damnit, Jeffrey. Play the applause—

[*Just then we hear a large, vault-sounding door kicked open. From what must be the entrance to the theater, we hear* CHER. *And she's pissed.*]

CHER:
STOP IN THE NAME OF LUNG POWER.

CARLA:
Cher?!

CHER:
That's right! Much like my 1987 hit, "I Found Someone," this time it's YOU, BITCH.

CARLA:
Jeffrey!

CHER:
I brought backup too!

[*We hear the voice of a different, older woman*: JOAN DIDION.]

JOAN DIDION:
"Sloughing Towards Babylon," are you fucking kidding me?

CARLA:
Joan Didion?!

JOAN DIDION:
You stole my entire essay. Except for that sick Charlie Manson shit.

CARLA:
Thank you. But how did you find me?!

JOAN DIDION:
Um, the marquee?

CHER:
"Carly Ronstadt: One Yight Nonly." [*A beat*] Like I said, I have dyslcxia.

CARLA:
Jeffrey, are you going to stop them or what?!

JEFFREY:
But they're national treasures, Miss Carla!

CHER:
We've teamed up like Cagney and Lacey! And we're here for PAYBACK! [*A beat*] How do bullets happen?

[CHER *cocks a shotgun.*]

Oh, there we go.

JOAN DIDION:
The center will not hold, clown.

CHAZ:
[*Walking in*] MOM, I'M HUNGRY.

CHER:
Chaz, get back in the car, honey!

CHAZ:
BUT, MOM—

CHER:
Help Auntie Didion untie these people while Mommy shoots the clown, then we'll get a McRib.

CHAZ:
OK.

JOAN DIDION:
There are innocent people here. Watch where you're pointing that thing.

CHER:
You know, I always used to say the same to Gregg Allman!

JEFFREY:
Miss Carla!

[*We hear an audience member tumble out of their seat.*]

AUDIENCE MEMBER:
I'm free! I'm FREE! And I'm calling the police on all you crazies!

CARLA:
Oh good luck, they're busy tear-gassing trans suffragettes!

JEFFREY:
Miss Carla!

CARLA:
Uh-oh.

AUDIENCE MEMBER:
911? 911! Yes, help! We've been abducted by a César Romero impersonator!

JEFFREY:
Miss Carla!

CARLA:
Um um um um um um.

JOAN DIDION:
Aim for the head, Cher.

CHER:
Say, Carla! Do you believe in life after love—I MEAN, shotgun blasts?

OTHER AUDIENCE MEMBER:
Get down! Get down!

CARLA:
Run, Jeffrey!

[*We hear multiple shotgun blasts, screams, things crashing, audience members screaming "my god, my god!" and* CARLA*'s clacking, panicked heels—and then the mic drops and hits the floor with a cracking impact. The sound of a tape spool running out. The text-to-speech voice from the beginning reads.*]

VOICE:
End of police evidence.

A click as the tape finally switches off.

A TALE AS OLD AS TIME; OR, IF YOU CAN'T BEAT 'EM, PLUNGE 'EM

(2023)

Carla Rossi in *Carla Rossi Does Drag*, 2023, at Reed College—with the members of the House of Elvira drag club joining her onstage. Photograph by Kate Bredeson.

The performance transcribed in this text was initially shared as part of *Carla Rossi Does Drag*, presented on January 25, 2023, at Reed College, produced by Kate Bredeson and the Reed College Department of Theatre.

Under the title *A Tale as Old as Time, or: If You Can't Beat 'Em, Plunge 'Em*, the resulting essay and transcription were published in National Performance Network's *Voices from the Network* artist blog on July 10, 2023.

A TALE AS OLD AS TIME; OR, IF YOU CAN'T BEAT 'EM, PLUNGE 'EM

(2023)

In 2018, I offered a drag queen storytime at the St. Johns Library in Portland, Oregon, that would eventually undo my life.

It was the most-attended drag queen storytime the city had seen at the time. More than one hundred youth and parents attended, making it a standing-room-only event. Dressed in my most child-friendly rainbow print dress as Portland's premier drag clown Carla Rossi, I read to children who could barely read on their own. I'm known for my whiteface makeup and satirical drag routines mocking whiteness in Portland, and I was worried the kids would be afraid of my clown face. But instead, they saw a person: one four-year-old remarked, "I love your lipstick!" as I sat down to read to her.

After the show, we moved to another room of the library for a dance party on bubble wrap. Dancing to Cher with a bunch of jumping toddlers, I lost my balance on the bubble wrap in my six-inch heels, and fell over, thanks in part to the kids excitedly bouncing off one another and into me. Embarrassed, I laughed to myself as Carla lay defeated and fallen, when a couple of the rowdiest kids jumped onto me in a pile. A librarian took a photo of us as their parents laughed and told them to climb off and help me up, and afterward we all went about our lives.

Within a few months, the photo—posted to a Flickr account by the library—caught the attention of conservative media, and before I knew it, my face and names were all over the Internet: misgendering me, calling me a pedophile, and condemning me, my career, and drag as a whole. I gained a QAnon following that still tracks and logs my in-person shows and social media activity, making dossiers about my "Satanic" behavior and cautionary videos about me and my friends using our own Instagram posts.

I forced myself to keep going and move on, continuing to host drag queen storytimes until the pandemic hit. I no longer offer them today. I still show up for drag engagements with Native youth, but that's yet to draw any conservative outrage. In an absolutely predictable twist, these folks don't pay attention to or care about Native kids, just white ones.

Still, it took years for me to comprehend the psychological impact of what happened: how children were wrongly sexualized and exploited by rabid strangers on the Internet in the name of destroying me and people like me. Today I feel a complicated mix of grief and shame that my drag queen storytime and the infamous photo have been used to fuel hatred to enact anti-trans legislation. Because, let's be real, the current "war on drag" is a coded war on trans people.

So, when it was time to present a new version of my touring greatest hits collection, Carla Rossi Does Drag, *at Reed College in January 2023, I found myself running on my treadmill and listening to previous mixes from old drag numbers when I heard a silly mix that mashed up "Beauty and the Beast" with "My Humps" for no reason other than its absurdity.*

Suddenly I had a vision: I realized that, since arguably one of Carla's greatest hits was her drag queen storytime from hell, I could turn it into an interactive drag number and incorporate screenshots of the horrible headlines while parodying exactly what conservatives pretend happens at a drag queen storytime in their worst fantasies. Creating this was one of the most terrifying things I've done in recent memory, but the audience was with me—as their screams of laughter and the look of mind-blown shock on my best friend's face demonstrated.

I didn't know it going in, but the process helped me perform something I'd needed desperately since that drag queen storytime at the St. Johns Library: an exorcism.

* * *

CARLA ROSSI *emerges from the wings in a stunning rainbow-print dress. She beams as she approaches her audience.*

How many of you have ever been to a drag queen storytime? How many of you have taken your children? Any kiddos that have been to drag queen storytimes? [*Seeing there is, in fact, a child in the audience*] Oh, you might want to close your eyes for this next part.

I actually became quite famous for my drag queen storytimes. And I would love to share it with you, if I could! For this, I just need some volunteers that are of age—that want to sit here and be the facsimile of children. [*Seeing some audience members raise their hands*] Yes, please, come down, come down! Let's welcome our friends.

[*The audience gives a round of applause as adult audience members approach* CARLA *onstage.*]

Yes, please sit. Look, I'm Chris Hansen: "I'm Chris Hansen, have a seat." [*As she greets each new audience participant, she mimics the host of "To Catch a Predator."*] Hi, I'm Chris Hansen, sit down. Hi, I'm Chris Hansen, sit down. Hi, I'm Chris Hansen, sit down. Hi, I'm Chris Haaaansen, sit down.

[*The audience participants sit beside her in a clump on the Marley floor.*]

Now, this is wonderful, but you did it all wrong. If you could spread out more, like an oval, so it's more pleasing for the audience to see me? And I'm just going to grab my book. Because you can't have a drag queen storytime without books!

[CARLA *shuffles offstage while the participants reshuffle their group into two parallel lines, parted like the Red Sea.* CARLA *reenters with a rolling chair and not a book.*]

Now you'll notice this is not a book, it's a chair. Because I like to multita—[*seeing the new formation they've taken onstage*]—oh, this is all wrong. Someone's been reading the Old Testament.

[*A new audience member takes a seat in between the two clusters, turning their formation into a U shape.* CARLA *smiles.*]

Look at that: a community-minded solution! [*A beat*] I don't want this chair.

[CARLA *exits with the rolling chair, finds a stationary chair with her children's book on it, and reenters with it. She plops her chair down in front of the onstage audience members.*]

OK, everyone. Now sit a little bit farther back, so you're not too close to me, because I'll get upset. And—hit it!

[*An instrumental version of "Beauty and the Beast," the title track of the musical, plays.* CARLA *smiles while holding* Cinders: A Chicken Cinderella *by Jan Brett. After the first few tinkling notes of piano,* CARLA *goes to sing.*]

Nope, it's a false start. [*A beat*] Walt Disney—you might not know this, kids—Walt Disney's a misogynist.

[*She waits for a few more tinkling notes from the piano before singing:*]

Tale as old as time
Song as old as—rust?
Maybe old as Darcelle*
Poison's† up there too
Anyway, the book—
Chicken Cinderella—
Will she end up gay?
I can't really say
I don't know how to read
drag queen storytime . . .

[*An abrupt record scratch followed by the bumping beats of "My Humps" by the Black Eyed Peas.* CARLA *begins to bump back and forth in her seat as she slowly opens the pages of the book with an elfish smile on her face. As she does so, a projection of the notorious image from* CARLA*'s real-life drag queen storytime slowly works its way up the back wall. It is massive.*

---

* Darcelle XV, Portland's longtime drag legend, Guinness World Record holder for oldest working drag queen performer and owner of Darcelle XV Showplace, passed away months after this performance on March 23, 2023, at age 92.

† Poison Waters, Darcelle's heir apparent and quintessential Portland drag icon.

Projection: *The infamous photo—*CARLA ROSSI, *splayed on the floor, kids on top of her, at the 2018 drag queen storytime at St. Johns Library.*

While Fergie sings "My Humps," CARLA *drops the book and begins to slowly raise the bottom of her dress, revealing her nude-tone legs and crotch (which are actually covered in three pairs of tights, two pairs of underwear, Spanx, a girdle, and foam padding). The audience onstage, watching like children at a storytime, giggle to each other and bounce back and forth on the floor. Just as a bell chimes in the song,* CARLA *drops the dress fabric back down to the floor, and the projected image zooms in to a close-up of her face before fading into a screenshot of a conservative news headline.*

Projection: *"CHILD ABUSE: Kids Lay on Man Dressed as a Woman at 'Drag Queen Story Time'—Alicia Powe." A colorful image of* CARLA *surrounded by floating, pearlescent soap bubbles is presented with it.*

Still bopping to the song, CARLA *begins to teasingly cross and uncross her legs like Sharon Stone in* Basic Instinct. *Another headline appears.*

Projection: *"LGTBQ agenda: Disgusting photos of kids lying on drag queens (photos): What is the next step? Disturbing photos from Portland, Oregon, show young children lying on top of a drag queen during a 'Drag Queen Story Time' event.* —Thema Newsroom." *The infamous library photo is shown with it.*

CARLA *swings herself to one side of the chair, sitting in profile and reclining back into the air, assuming a pose like Liza Minnelli's Sally Bowles in* Cabaret. *She kicks her legs up and down in the air. Then at another chime in the song, another headline*:

Projection: *"Child Abuse Update! Library Caught Allowing Tots to Roll Around with Drag Demons! —Roy Batty,* The Daily Stormer." *A still of* CARLA *from the Seattle Art Museum's popular video of Carla interacting with Jeffrey Gibson's* Like a Hammer *exhibition.*

CARLA *gets up from her chair and shimmies into an onstage audience participant. She begins grinding up and down behind their head, facing away from them—and not even making contact. It's not sexy, but* CARLA *thinks it might be in some universe. The song chimes again.*

Projection: *Zooming in on* The Daily Stormer *article: "I think we're all just waiting at this point to hear the inevitable headline, 'Demonic Tranny Drag Queen Crossdresser Opens Portal to Hell, Sucks in Children.'"*

Still as unsexy and arhythmic as ever, CARLA *tries working her way down three onstage audience participants, bopping her butt up and down near the back of their heads. The song chimes again.*

Projection: *"Shocking photos: kids lie on man dressed as woman at Drag Queen Story Time* —LifeSiteNews.com." *The infamous library photo is presented again with this headline.*

CARLA *dances her way back to her stationary chair center stage, and pulls it further upstage. The song goes into a bridge.*

Projection: *"Photos of children lying on top of drag queen at 'storytime' event allegedly taken down by library after images called out.* —TheBlaze." *With the subhead: "I wouldn't let my kids crawl on top of strangers." The still of* CARLA *from the Seattle Art Museum video is reused.*

CARLA *marches over to something hidden in the shadows downstage right: a plunger.* CARLA *returns center stage with the plunger, and the projected image changes to:*

Projection: *"Creepy photos show kids laying on top of drag queen.* —Summit News." *With the subhead: "Pictures removed from library website after events revealed." The first paragraph of the story is visible: "The photos were posted by the Multnomah County Library's Flickr account but were swiftly removed once* Life Site News *drew attention to them." A second, different photo of* CARLA *from the storytime event.*

CARLA *shuffle-steps slightly downstage and grandly slams the plunger onto the ground, suctioning it to the floor just as Fergie lets out an "oooooh" in the song.*

Projection: *"LIBRARY DELETES PHOTOS OF CHILDREN FONDLING DRAG QUEENS DURING 'STORY HOUR.'* —Breitbart."

CARLA *wobbles her feet to line up directly on either side of the plunger, then begins to raise her dress to her knees. She drops the dress over the plunger, concealing it altogether, and dances in place with her hands in her hair.*

Projection: *A pixilated meme shows several photos, clockwise from left: Cheddar Gorgeous wearing only a necklace and a silver codpiece and posing with a child in drag;* CARLA *with kids collapsed on her from the library; a young boy, sitting on one male parent's shoulders, kissing his other male parent, while walking in a Pride parade; an image of Violet Chachki presumably in a merkin or codpiece, with her lower half pixelated to make her appear nude while posing with a child; at center, a poorly drawn spiral with the caption: "LBLogo aka 'Little Boy Lover.'" Beginning at the top of the image and running to the bottom are the words: "The LGBT's motives / Couldn't be more clear."*

Still dancing in place, CARLA *slooowly lowers herself down, and down, and down—kneeling directly where the plunger should be.*

Then, just as Fergie sings "Make you scream, make you scream," CARLA, *still kneeling, grabs a mic and lets out a banshee cry. She screams with a shell-shocked look in her eyes. The projected image explodes. Another record scratch.*

"Beauty and the Beast" resumes.

CARLA *stands and backs away from the plunger, which her dress gets caught on, before trying to pick it up despite its being hermetically stuck to the floor. Instead, the plunger's wood handle breaks off in her hand, and she stares at it before throwing it across the floor.*]

[*singing*] Tale as old as time
Song as old as—rust?
What will happen to the chicken?
Will she marry the prince?
Drag queen storytime

[CARLA *takes her place back on the chair with her book, still singing.*]

Tale as old as time
Song as old as—

[CARLA *falls silent instead of singing the last verse. She stares blankly at the audience, shaken, empty, her eyes wide, mouth hanging open, as the song ends. We hear the final tinkles of the piano as she speaks to those gathered around her.*]

Now go home, children—go home and be weaponized by strangers on the Internet.

[CARLA *stands up and exits like there's no tomorrow.*]